Jennifer survived the Boston Marathon bombing, but this isn't a book about that. Each one of us are survivors in the maze of life, and need inspiring stories like hers to lead us out. She is among the greats of our generation, alongside speakers and authors like Nick Vujicic and other inspiring world changers.

Tammy Kling, *TEDx speaker, bestselling author, founder,*
The Conversation Ceo, OnFire Books

This book will encourage you to trust more, believe deeper and reach higher. Jennifer shares her struggles honestly and the reader is encouraged to find their significance in a relationship with Jesus Christ.

Becky Hyde, *CEO Metroplex Women's Clinic*

Many years ago I adopted the mantra of an older friend (not a runner) who said, "The day I spot someone running with a smile on their face is the day I take up running." That mantra kept me out of the race for years... until I spotted my friend Jennifer McAlister running through our neighborhood. The writers of Scripture often compared life to a long race filled with distractions, obstacles, setbacks, and tragedy. Sometimes it feels like survival is the best we can hope for.

Whether you're a fierce competitor or only thinking about thinking about getting off the sofa someday, *Press On* will encourage you to something better than surviving. This book is filled with honest stories of both struggle and victory that will inspire you to stare down the course marked out for you, turn your attention toward Jesus, and press on toward a life of joy, courage, and hope. I heartily recommend it to you.

Chris Freeland, *Lead Pastor, McKinney Church*

Loved the book! It's real! Great read. Easy read. I loved the stories in it and the faith from it. I felt like I was in it. Great descriptions of Jennifer's experiences with poignant insights to strengthen the reader. I believe this book is going to encourage many people. Congratulations on the high level of excellence and may many, many more of these follow.

Jeff Klingenberg, *Lead Pastor, Highridge Church*

Two of my favorite faith topics: perseverance and trust are thoroughly explored in Jennifer McAlister's book *Press On*. If you want to understand how boldness and humility go together, how strength and weakness are at once the same and how pain can feel so good then build time into your workout schedule to read this book.

In describing the role trust plays in our daily pursuit of life she says, "If we really want to see the power of God it has to be personal and we have to be in a place where we need it." Her writing lacks complicated platitudes—this is simple and clear perspective you can use now.

Jennifer brings a tone to her writing that goes way beyond insightful and compelling. She says, "I want to honor Him by living with purpose, boldness and a sense of urgency." That's the hallmark of someone who's truly learned how to trust in God alone. Each chapter in *Press On* delivers tough truths from a spirit of total abandon. If that sounds extremely robust, it is in an exceptionally intimate way. Jennifer doesn't just let you hear her conversations with God—You get to experience the living dialogue God has with her. She says, "This word brings me to my knees." And it will for you too.

Trust me! This book will press you to take a fresh look at how you pursue your goals, live your dreams and listen to God.

Brad Bloom, *Publisher, Faith & Fitness Magazine,*
FaithAndFitness.net

Press On is invigorating words on a page! More than words it is a collection of stories of perseverance and a deep developed trust in an unshakeable God who is on control of all things. This book will inspire you to put your trust in the One who is able to safely bring us to our final destination! Jennifer will encourage you to press forward and live life with eternity in mind.

Debbie Brown *is on staff at Houston's First Baptist Church and has been joyfully leading the Fitness Ministry for 20 years*

Let this book motivate, accelerate, and encourage you to press on in faith as you trust God in every area of your life. An easy read full of inspiration in easily swallowed doses. Highly recommend!

The Benham Brothers
Authors, Speakers, and Entrepreneurs

PRESS
ON

*Stories of endurance, faith,
and trust to encourage you
as you run the race of life*

JENNIFER MCALISTER

Carpenter's Son Publishing

Press On

Published by Carpenter's Son Publishing, Franklin, Tennessee

Published in association with Larry Carpenter of Christian Book Services, LLC

www.christianbookservices.com

Interior Design by Adept Content Solutions

Cover Design by Jennifer McAlister

Edited by Tammy Kling, Mary K. Hoch, Jeanne Hoch

ISBN 978-1-942587-84-2

Printed in the United States of America

For Jason, Marissa, Savanna,
Skyler, Jace and Canon

So let us know, let us press on to know the Lord...
(Hosea 6:3)

I press on toward the goal to win the prize for which
God has called me heavenward in Christ Jesus.
(Philippians 3:14)

Contents

Foreword

Who do you trust? We never really have the opportunity to think about these things until we're in the midst of a storm or until faith is tested. A broken relationship, loss of a loved one, or an issue with your finances may have you reaching out for someone to lean on or a friend who could offer you wisdom, but it can be difficult to know who to confide in. In our darkest hour, who do we trust?

I believe the greatest compliment in the world is trust. When someone trusts you, they believe you are reliable, good, and honest. The Merriam-Webster Dictionary defines trust as "assured reliance on the character, ability, strength, or truth of someone or something." But you don't need a formal definition to understand what trust actually feels like. Trust is a lot like love. You know it when you feel it, and you know it when you don't—even if you can't understand why. When your trust is violated, it feels like the biggest betrayal in the world. However, when you find someone who continually invites you to trust them—and they can back it up—you feel safe and secure.

Do you trust easily? I don't think I did. Many of the stories in this book involve trust. It didn't come naturally for me, so I had to be put in situations where I had no choice but to trust. I've often said that God speaks to us in what we know, so I was taught many lessons that applied to life while training for endurance events. I guess that makes sense since life often feels like a race—times when our strength is gone, we are too tired to keep moving, and we wonder where the finish line is.

Like everything else, in order for us to be good at something, we have to practice. I've often prayed for my faith and trust to increase, but in order to get it, I needed some classroom time, which is what most of the stories in this book are about: persistence, endurance, and trust.

Trust can be hard to embrace for a lot of us because we live in a broken world surrounded by imperfect people. We are shocked when friends let us down, tragedies occur, and our troubles seem never-ending. But let's face it; broken things aren't supposed to work right. Yet, in all this, we can have peace knowing that nothing takes God by surprise. I read a quote by Adrian Rogers that said, "Has it ever occurred to you that nothing ever occurs to God?" He is able to turn all things around for good for those who love Him and not just some things, but all things. The problem is we want to experience God's miracles, but we don't want to be in a place where we need one. We want our faith and trust to increase, but we don't want to go through the necessary training.

The Bible tells the story of Moses and the Israelites, who were in a bad place; they had the Egyptians behind them and the Red Sea in front of them, and they were out of options. But—they were right in the center of God's will. They would not have been able to witness His mighty power to separate the waters had they not been in an impossible situation.

How can we personally know that God is trustworthy and has the ability, strength, and power to solve our biggest problems if we never have any?

As I look back, I realize I trust and love God so much because He has proven to be faithful in the hardest times of my life. I wouldn't want to go through those challenging times again, but I am so grateful for all that I learned during them. I experienced an intimacy with Christ that is only found when we share in His sufferings. In Philippians 3:10, the Apostle Paul says it this way, ". . . I want to know Him and the power of His resurrection and the fellowship of His sufferings."

If we really want to see the power of God, it has to be personal, and we have to be in a place where we need it.

Years ago I was at my youngest daughter's softball practice when we had to leave quickly because a tornado was heading in our direction. We rushed home and hid in the laundry room. The room was dark, the wind was howling, and we were helpless. We were at the mercy of something that we didn't cause or ask for, and all we could do was pray that God would protect us. After about twenty minutes, the storm passed, and we were able to exit the dark room that held us, grateful it was over.

The next morning, I was driving my girls to school when my youngest daughter said, "Mommy, I thanked God for the storm last night."

I looked at her in the rearview mirror and asked, "Why did you thank Him for a storm? You were so scared."

Her mature answer still reminds of me of how I need to look at difficulties in my life when she said in a matter of fact way: "Well sometimes I get busy playing with my Barbie dolls, my toys, or my friends, and I forget about God. But last night when the storm was loud and the room was dark, I never forgot Him. I was talking to Him all night. So I thanked Him for the storm."

C. S. Lewis said, "God whispers to us in our pleasures but He screams at us on in our pain." When things are going good, we have a tendency to wander and, like my daughter said, forget about God. However, when we find ourselves in hopeless situations, our despair should cause us to look up and cry to the only One who can save us. I've often said that Satan must be the most frustrated entity in the universe because every plan of his gets turned around for good the moment we turn to God and put our trust in Him. In fact, he may not even be happy when horrible things happen because he knows it won't be long before we cry out to Jesus. I think he prefers for us to walk apathetically through life, never having any major problems and never needing God.

When we have this perspective, we can be thankful even for trials because they serve a greater purpose. Unfortunately, not everyone will do this. There is no denying that life can be hard; we have no control over that. What we do have control over is how we react to it. Will we become bitter or better? When we put our trust in God, even when we don't understand, we will become better. He moves us from faith to faith, and as He does, our trust in Him increases. We get to enter into His rest and have a supernatural peace in spite of our circumstances. We may not know why things happen, but we know who is in control, and we can rely on his character, ability, and strength to handle any situation.

I was at a Bible study recently, and one of the questions asked was, "On a scale of one to ten, how would you rate your faith?" When it comes to trusting God, I would say ten—He has never let me down. The problem that has gotten me into trouble is that I don't trust myself and therefore fall into a works-based trap without even realizing it. Many people have done the same thing at one time or another. We pick up burdens we were never intended to carry and beat ourselves up over bad choices we've made. We experience the ache of regret, we doubt our abilities, we question our decisions, and we punish ourselves over the would have, should have, could haves in our life. I have been guilty of this more times than I can count. When I am disappointed in myself, I mistakenly believe that God must be disappointed in me as well. Then I read a beautiful verse in the Bible that said I was standing in grace.

"We have gained access by faith into this grace in which we now stand. And we boast in the hope of the glory of God" (Romans 5:2). Grace is undeserved. Grace is a gift from God, and by faith I needed to understand that God knows everything I have done and everything I will do and loves me anyway. Donald Miller said it best in his book *Scary Close*: "Grace only sticks to our imperfections. If we can't accept our imperfections, we can't accept grace."

I am standing in grace. If you trust in Jesus, you are standing in grace. We don't need to add to what He has already accomplished at the cross. When we continue to beat ourselves up over past mistakes and regrets, we are in effect saying that what He did wasn't enough. The reality is there is nothing more we can add. Jesus told us, "It is finished." He paid a fine we could never pay and we shouldn't even try. In every other situation, do we worry about a bill or fine that someone has already taken care of?

I read a story about a man who was about to be engulfed by the angry flames of a forest fire, so he ran to the safety of a burned down house to escape a certain death. The destruction of the house was so complete that everything that could burn had been consumed. The house could not catch on fire twice because there was nothing left; all the fuel had been spent! The same is true with what Jesus did for us at the cross—He took our punishment to the full, so there is nothing left to burn—not past sins, future sins, or regret. The judgment was so complete there is nothing we can add to the fire of God's wrath. It is finished. We are standing in grace (God's Riches At Christ's Expense). Why do we make the mistake of trying to drag wood and kindling to a place where judgment has already occurred—it would serve no purpose! Worse than that, it doesn't honor God's sacrifice on our behalf. What does is when we thank and trust Him for allowing us to stand in the safety of His grace.

I pray as you read this book, your trust in God increases as you see Him in every situation of your life—the good, the bad, the big, and the small through your hobbies, your kids, your job, and even your day-to-day routines. I've learned the most on my seemingly insignificant days because every day is significant to Him. Yes, we live in an imperfect world, but we have a perfect God, who reminds us that the even the eagle needs turbulence in order to rise above and soar.

Chapter 1

Mile 26.1—
2013 Boston Marathon

I survived the Boston Marathon, not just the race but the race the year that there was an unexpected bombing that claimed the lives of spectators and runners and severely wounded many forever.

Looking back now, I realize how every second of that day was significant and made the difference between life and death. On this side of eternity, it's hard to see how good can come from tragedy, but our view is limited. My heart still hurts for the families of those who lost a loved one, and I pray they have peace, knowing their sacrifice was not in vain. God will never waste their tears, and He promises to be close to the brokenhearted. As for me, I got to experience up close and personal how quickly our lives can be taken. We aren't promised tomorrow, or even the next second for that matter.

Every day is a gift, and since God chose to keep me around for a little while longer, I want to honor Him by living with purpose, boldness, and a sense of urgency. I pray He will continue to teach me to number my days so I can present to Him a heart of wisdom.

When I think of the bystanders who were killed and all those who were injured, it breaks my heart. Our whole world can change in one moment, and that moment makes all the difference. I found the things that were so important to me before the Boston Marathon meant nothing to me after the explosion. That morning, my biggest concern was how fast I could run my race; after the bomb, I was concerned about whether I would ever see my husband, family, and friends again. Tragedy has a way of realigning your priorities.

On the day we started that race, I felt nothing but exhilaration and joy but after running over twenty six miles, I was ready to be done. Overwhelmed with emotion, I stared down the street leading to the finish line for the Boston Marathon. The joy of seeing a dream become a reality, the relief of finishing, and the anticipated excitement of greeting my husband Jason at the finish line kept my feet moving. I normally speed up when I can see the finish, but on that day, my legs could barely shuffle. All I wanted was to be done, get my medal, and sit down. I was exhausted, and I couldn't wait for the relief of resting. That's when I heard a loud boom. I was at mile 26.1, close to completing my marathon, so I didn't stop running. I saw smoke at the finish line but wasn't close enough to understand what it was from. Surely it was something innocent, Patriot's Day fireworks, perhaps? As I continued to run forward, the building right in front of me shot into flames and thick smoke billowed into the street. The loud blast, fire, and screams of bystanders made it clear that we were under attack.

I felt paralyzed as I watched helplessly as people were frantically running away from the finish line. The finish line was where my husband and friends were.

A police officer started shouting at me to get away from the trash can. When I saw the fear and panic in the officer's eyes, I realized that this was serious and braced myself for the next detonation. Yet in this moment, I realized that I was not afraid to die. I didn't want to be separated from my family, but I felt at peace—God was in control. Because I had accepted Jesus as my Savior, I knew that I would immediately be with Him if He chose to take me home. What I was afraid of was the pain of getting there!

Silently I prayed that if another bomb went off and hit me, it would be quick, painless, and complete. When nothing happened for a few moments, I tried to make my way to the finish line. True panic now started to set in. I knew Jason and my friends were all supposed to be there. Was my husband alive, was he hurt? Were my friends okay? My mind raced and my heart pounded. As I tried to get to them, I was turned back by police officers who were not allowing anyone near the devastation.

Qualifying for the Boston Marathon had been a goal, dream, and prayer for my friends Toni, Chimene and me for years. However, in order to register for Boston, we each needed to finish a marathon in less than three hours and forty-five minutes. After many attempts and disappointments in 2011, I began to entertain the thought that it might not happen for me.

The following year, we all decided to run the St. George Marathon. It was my idea, and I asked Toni if she would sign up with me. She agreed, and both of us registered online. The St. George marathon uses the lottery system, so not everyone who registers is guaranteed a spot. Lo and behold, Toni was accepted, and I wasn't. "When you get a 'no,' it is because a greater 'yes' is coming," kept going through my mind.

In the middle of the night, I woke up with the solution— fundraise! If I raised money for a charity, I would be guaranteed a spot in the marathon. I believe this was God's plan all along. I chose to raise money for the Dove Center in Utah that helps families harmed by domestic violence. I had lost my dear friend, Shelby, to domestic violence, and I wanted to honor her memory as well as help other women. This endeavor wasn't without great contemplation. Shelby had called me on a Thursday evening, and I didn't answer because I was busy. She left me a message and said she needed to talk to me. I had to be somewhere that weekend, so I didn't call her back until Sunday morning—ten minutes after her husband shot her. For a long time it was my greatest regret. Why hadn't I returned her call? What if I could have made a difference? I realized that I couldn't change the past, but I could do something in the present and make a difference now, so fundraising at the Dove Center was what I would do.

Due to the generosity of my family and friends, I not only raised enough money for my entry but also for my friend, Chimene. A greater 'yes' indeed!

The three of us, dressed in matching outfits and ready to run, began the St. George Marathon feeling strong. Toni and I ran ahead of Chimene, who decided to run with the pace group. We were running faster than we needed to but didn't realize it because we felt so great. I kept up with Toni until we reached the dreaded hill that greets you at mile nine and doesn't say goodbye until mile thirteen. I was very happy that I held a faster pace in the beginning because I was losing speed on the hills. There were times when I was hurting and wanted to quit, but then I would think, this pain is nothing compared to what Shelby's family has had to endure—do this for her. That kept me going.

I then began to focus on one simple goal: put one foot in front of the other. That can be difficult to do when you're physically taxed and running a race. Sometimes you just want to give up. Psalm 121 was my saving verse when the pain would intensify. "I lift my eyes to the hills, from where does my help come from? My help comes from the Lord, the Maker of Heaven and Earth." Before I knew it, I was at the top of the hill with a beautiful view one can only see from that vantage point. Thank you, Lord!

Unfortunately, Toni was nowhere in sight. Because of what I had learned from my previous marathons, I didn't get too discouraged because I had a lot of time to catch her. I chose not to stop at every water stop to make up for my slower pace on the hills, and it paid off. At mile 23, I looked ahead of me and saw the same outfit I was wearing! It was Toni, and I was overjoyed! I ran up behind her, tapped her on the shoulder, and by God's grace, we had the joy of finishing the marathon together. Not only did we qualify for Boston but with five minutes to spare! Toni and I anxiously waited for Chimene at the finish line. We all wanted to qualify and prayed that God would allow that to happen. We didn't have to wait long; only three minutes later, we saw her triumphantly cross the finish line where we hugged and cried together. All three of us were Boston qualifiers!

Finally the highly anticipated weekend arrived, and we didn't waste a minute of the experience. The three runners, along with my husband, Jason, and Chimene's husband, Arnold, had fun taking pictures, touring the city, and shopping at the expo. I had the joy of finally being able to officially wear the Boston Marathon jacket and kept it on most of the time. All the hours of training and the many miles our running shoes had traveled were worth this feeling of accomplishment. As Proverbs 13:19 says, "A desire fulfilled is sweet to the soul."

Jason and Arnold planned on meeting us at certain spots along the marathon course. Jason pointed out an area near the finish line that he thought would be a great place to watch us finish. I kept this spot in mind so I would know where to find them the next day.

We were set to start at 10:20, so we didn't have to get up as early as usual. Toni and I met Chimene at the starting area and decided to use the restroom one last time before our 26.2 mile adventure began. The line was not moving fast, and I had a very uneasy feeling. We missed our 10:20 start, putting us behind. Once we began running, I forgot all about my uneasiness. I was wrapped up in the moment and thrilled to be taking part in something that seemed beyond my reach for so many years.

Toni and I started out fast while Chimene decided to hold back. For the first thirteen miles, we felt great and then we hit the dreaded wall. We both started hurting at around the same time.

"Let's not worry about it," I told Toni, "we're not running this to qualify but to enjoy the accomplishment of being here. Let's just have fun."

Like always, we were wearing matching outfits. Our shirts read "Soul Sisters, Sole Sisters" on the front, and a scripture was on the back. We chose Galatians 6:14 for this race: "May I never boast except in the cross of our Lord Jesus Christ, through which the world has been crucified to me, and I to the world."

At mile 15, we saw Team Hoyt ahead of us. Team Hoyt is a father-and-son team, who participate in both marathons and triathlons. The son has cerebral palsy, so his father pushes him in special wheelchair while they run. It was so motivating for me to see them at this particular point in the race. How could I complain about being tired when this amazing man was pushing his grown son in a wheelchair? Seeing them also reminded me of how our Heavenly Father carries us when we can't do it by ourselves—not because He has to but because He loves us. Toni and I asked if they would take a picture with us, and they graciously did. The entire exchange took about forty-five seconds, but it was worth it. I call these types of moments kisses from God. Life can be very hard sometimes, and He knows we need to be refreshed as we run the race of life.

At around mile 20, Chimene caught up with us and passed. Her plan to take it easy in the beginning paid off, and she was now ahead. Toni and I had planned on staying together until we crossed the finish line. Unfortunately, Toni stopped momentarily at around mile 25 because her stomach hurt, but I didn't know it. She was calling my name, but I had my headphones in and didn't hear her. I kept going and found myself turning onto Boylston Street without her.

That's when the blast came.

"Please, can I use your phone?" I cried to a spectator on the route.

I dialed Jason's cell phone, and all I heard was "beep, beep, beep." My heart jumped into my throat.

"Please Lord, let him be okay! Please Lord, please Lord."

I hit redial twice before I heard the beautiful sound.

"Hello."

"Oh, thank God," I cried into the phone.

"We got stuck in traffic. We couldn't make it to the finish line," he told me. "And don't worry, Chimene is okay, too."

Panic and confusion continued to reign as emergency workers pushed us away from the finish line. In less than five minutes, I had experienced so many emotions: exhaustion, euphoria, joy, confusion, fear, panic, terror, relief, and then nothing. I was numb.

I watched in shock as hundreds of emergency vehicles passed me and helicopters hovered overhead. Cold and confused, I wandered up the street, not knowing where to go or what to do. As the authorities pushed us further away from the crime scene, I encountered a group of men who surrounded me.

"What happened?" one of the men asked me.

"Bombs exploded at the finish line." I replied.

He didn't seem shocked. "Did you finish?"

"No," I said.

"I told you she wouldn't finish!" Another man piped up.

"What is going on?" I wondered. "I don't know these men. Why would he say that? How could he know how badly that statement hurt? I have to get away from them." I pushed past them and started moving further up Boylston Street. It was such a random comment from a random stranger. It was almost as if the devil had whispered in his ear, "I told you she wouldn't finish."

Then I remembered a verse from Ephesians 6:12 that said, "For our struggle is not against flesh and blood, but against the rulers, against the authorities, against the powers of this dark world and against the spiritual forces of evil in the heavenly realms." That verse was a game changer. Suddenly I was approached by another stranger who started challenging me about the scripture on the back of my shirt.

"What does your Bible say about women preaching?" he yelled at me.

"I am not preaching," I replied.

"What church do you go to? Where are you from?" He kept bombarding me with questions and accusations.

My mind was reeling. Was this for real? People were dead and injured less than a mile away from us, and he was harassing me over my t-shirt? It's like I was stuck in a bad dream and couldn't wake up.

"You need to go away," I told him, but he didn't listen.

All of this odd spiritual warfare was occurring at the exact moment that lives were being lost. Have you ever had something so strange and unexplainable occur in your own life? I've learned that when things don't make sense, there's a reason. Then another man approached us. "You need to go," he told the obnoxious stranger with authority.

Thankfully the man didn't argue but simply said, "Okay" and walked away. As belligerent as he was, I was amazed that he didn't argue or try to get the last word in. He simply left. The kind man stayed with me and didn't leave my side—it must have been obvious that I needed help. He let me use his phone to text Jason. My hands shook so badly that I couldn't type, so the man typed for me. We exchanged many texts with Jason as we tried to figure out where to meet. The man finally told Jason that he would take me to a hotel close by and Jason could meet us there.

The man walked me to the hotel where I thanked him for his help. We said goodbye. I was an emotional mess, distraught and untethered.

The hotel lobby was thick with tension and fear as people were anxiously trying to locate family members and friends while at the same time wondering when the next blast would be. As I stood in the crowded lobby, I watched as people were reunited with loved ones and witnessed the look of relief on their faces as they hugged and cried. They were given a gift, and they were appreciating it to the fullest. I knew Jason was okay because I had spoken to him, but until I had him with me, I couldn't rest—it really felt like I was in a war zone. Why was it taking him so long? My mind started playing the "what if" game, and I found my eyes glued to the door waiting for him to arrive. It worked as well as waiting for water to boil, but I couldn't help it. While standing at the window, I watched as the streets of Boston continued to fill with emergency vehicles, their sirens an eerie reminder of the seriousness of the situation. Looking up, more helicopters were hovering overhead, all on high alert, just like everyone surrounding me in the lobby as we nervously waited for what was to come.

Just before Jason arrived, I saw the kind man standing in the corner. I thought he had left, but I wonder now if he was waiting for Jason to arrive. I was so happy to see Jason when he walked into the hotel lobby. After today, I realize all the more that we are not promised tomorrow, and the thought of almost losing him made me want to hold him tight and not let go.

Later in the evening, I asked Jason to text the man who so graciously helped me, and let him know how appreciative we were.

"That's a good idea," Jason said, and he took out his phone. After a few minutes of scrolling through his phone, he seemed perplexed.

"I can't find any of the texts from him," Jason replied. "There is nothing here."

Jason hadn't erased anything, and he knew the exact time the texts were sent, but they weren't there. Messages from others that were sent before and after their exchange were there, but there was absolutely no record of the multiple texts sent back and forth between them.

This man showed up when I needed him and helped me when I couldn't help myself. The Bible tells us in Hebrews 1:14 that angels are ministering spirits sent to serve those who will inherit salvation.

If ever I needed an angel, it was then, so I wouldn't be surprised if I someday find out that he was indeed an angel from heaven! Whether he was a Good Samaritan or an actual angel, I will be forever grateful. He helped me in one of my darkest hours.

Finally, we were all reunited at Chimene and Arnold's hotel. The media began calling and interviewing us about our experiences since we were so close to the explosions. From *Sports Illustrated* to our local newspapers, interviews were abundant. The first call came less than five hours after the initial blast.

"Hello," I said, my voice cracking a bit.

"Hello, this is a reporter from the *Star Telegram*. Can I ask you a few questions?

His questions were ones that were asked many times over the course of the next few months: "What was is like being so close to the bombs? What was going through your head when you realized this was an attack? Were you worried more bombs were going to go off?"

When I responded to him, I spoke in the past tense but was still living the answer in the present tense,

"I was scared. I was in disbelief; I was in shock. I can't understand how such evil could occur on a day that was supposed to be full of joy and accomplishment. I don't know why I was spared and others weren't."

It all seemed so surreal. We were sick over what happened to the precious bystanders, who were there simply to support others, and angered over the evil that seemed to prevail on what should have been a perfect day.

* * *

It took about three days before the numb feeling began to subside. It was like anesthesia wearing off, and I started to feel all the emotions I should have had immediately following the explosions. I felt nervous and irritable. My heart rate was elevated, and even the simplest of tasks seemed overwhelming. I began to question why God would allow this, while at the same time praising Him for His hand of protection over us. I reflected on how close we all came to being killed or injured.

Had Toni and I not stopped to take a picture with Team Hoyt, I would have been directly in front of the second blast when the bombs exploded (The Boston Marathon Association later emailed me my estimated finish time based on where I was the 40K mark. The first bomb exploded at 4:09:43. My estimated finish time was 4:09:36). So many things had to happen exactly as they did for us all to be safe. Even Jason and Arnold—had they not been caught in traffic or had Chimene lingered at the finished line . . .

I am so grateful that we were all protected, but at the same time I feel guilty for being upset at not being able to cross the finish line. I struggle to understand why God wanted me to be at this marathon at this particular time. It took twelve marathons before I qualified for Boston, years of prayers, hundreds of hours of training, and finally a miracle from God Himself to get me there.

Why would I be stopped at mile 26.1? The answer was spoken to my heart a few days after I began questioning God.

"This is just an intermission. You will come back and cross the finish line. But because of your testimony, you will be able to cross the eternal finish line, holding hands with many other souls."

This word brought me to my knees. Oh let it be! Only a great and awesome God can take something so horrific and bring good out of it. The cross is a perfect example of how He turns *all* things around for good for those who love Him and are called according to His purpose. I will continue to share my story, pleading with all who will listen that we are not promised tomorrow. My prayer is that everyone in my sphere of influence will understand that Jesus is the only way and accept His gift of salvation before it is too late. We never know when a bomb might blow.

* * *

The struggles in your life may never be as tragic as a terrorist attack, and I pray they aren't. In fact, you may live a life of peace and joy and love without any major problems at all. Regardless of what state you are in, I pray my story will encourage you to take 2 Corinthians 6:2 to heart, for God says, "At just the right time, I heard you. On the day of salvation, I helped you." Indeed, the "right time" is now. Today is the day of salvation.

He is only a prayer away.

Pause and Reflect

- We are not promised tomorrow. Do you know where you will spend eternity?

Chapter 2

Pick Your Pain

Throughout my life I have been advised by many a non-runner about how horrible running is on the body. Some of the more popular warnings I have received are:

"You will ruin your knees."

"All that pounding the pavement is dangerous."

"You won't be able to enjoy life when you get older because of the damage you are causing with all this running . . ." and the list goes on.

I find it ironic that those who are the quickest to counsel me on the dangers of running are those who have an aversion to exercise. Never mind that I've seen men and women in their eighties passing me during races, or whole families, including grandma and grandpa, celebrating life by running a race together. The significance of running a race is far more than just running the race. The motivation behind the race is different for everyone: the loss of a loved one, a success, reaching a weight-loss goal, running to beat cancer or in memory of someone who didn't, or just simply family bonding or connecting with a group of friends. Running a race takes commitment.

Even if you're an everyday avid runner and have no intention of competing in a race, you understand that running isn't just something you want to do; for many of us it's something we have to do. For some runners, running is a mental release and a way of clearing the head. Running provides a sense of comfort when you get in your zone, perhaps in the same way ballet may feel to a dancer or journaling to a writer. The pain of not running would be far greater than the pain of running each day, feeling the wind on your face and racing down winding roads or forest-lined trails. But to the non-runner—we might look crazy.

"The only time you'll catch me running is if a bear is chasing me!" I've heard people say, shaking their heads. They just don't get it. And that's okay.

I've thought many a time on how I should respond to their well-meaning (though not always accurate) advice, and I think I've finally come up with the answer—"Pick your pain."

We will all suffer from some form of pain, exercise-induced or not. For me, the aching feet and sore muscles after a long run are a small price to pay for the health benefits gained. Inactive people may not experience this but could very possibly suffer from the consequences of a sedentary lifestyle: obesity, heart disease, and high blood pressure—just to name a few. This pain is far more dangerous, so I choose the pain that provides the better alternative. Even athletes who go to the gym and feel that they're in their comfort zone there often don't understand runners. But athletes run. Every major sport requires movement, and whether you're a baseball player, soccer player, or a hockey player, you still need to run and have a healthy heart. If you're not an athlete, you need some form of cardio to keep your heart healthy and your body strong.

"Pick your pain" is something I say to myself every day. I realized a long time ago that I hate the feeling of being out of shape more than I hate going to the gym or going for a run. Therefore, I pick my pain. As much as I love exercising and running, if you are pushing yourself, you will feel discomfort. No one ever remained healthy sitting on the couch.

Getting up early to work out while everyone is sleeping is painful, but the results of an active lifestyle are very rewarding. Physically, I have found that the body becomes very efficient when you are a runner, and it doesn't want to carry more weight than it has to—so maintaining my goal weight is a benefit. Emotionally, the joy of crossing a finish line after a hard race far exceeds the pain of getting to the finish line. One of my favorite quotes says, "The pain of discipline or the pain of regret—you choose." The pain of discipline is temporary; the pain of regret is lifelong. Temporary pain is the much wiser choice!

Picking your pain doesn't just apply to the running world but also to society as a whole. If everyone understood that there is no such thing as a "pain-free" route in life, we wouldn't have the entitlement mentality that is becoming more and more prevalent in today's world. Starting a business is hard, getting an education takes discipline, being a good parent takes endurance and patience, and achieving goals takes commitment, but, oh, the reward is so great and desire realized is sweet to the soul (Proverbs 13:19).

The road to success, happiness, and fulfillment is the road less traveled because it is the hardest route to take. Only those who understand the consequences of the alternative dare to step foot on this path. It can be hot, hilly, and at times treacherous. Ironically, those on this journey are happier than their flatland counterparts who chose the seemingly easier route. They have come to realize that there is joy in the midst of pain. They have learned that faith, hope, goals, dreams, and purpose provide strength to put one foot in front of the other, and the journey becomes an adventure.

What the easy road travelers don't understand is that a pain-free life doesn't exist. The more they try to avoid "doing hard things," the harder their lives become. The Bible reminds us that there is profit in all labor, but mere talk leads only to poverty. Profit is the reward for labor (physical or mental exertion, especially when difficult or exhausting; work). Poverty is the reward for trying to avoid pain. I feel so sorry for those who take this path because they will never know the joys of accomplishment or the rewards of hard work.

When you wake up tomorrow morning, you will have a decision to make. Will you make a commitment to work hard on your mind, body, and family and even step outside of your comfort zone if you need to? Leaders lead others through the journey of getting stronger and better each day. It's never too late to teach your kids or others around you how to reach for high goals and continually establish higher expectations.

My advice to you is pick your pain, don't avoid it, understand that it's a part of life, and be ready to confront it head on, like a warrior.

"I consider that our present sufferings are not worth comparing with the glory that will be revealed in us."
(Romans 8:18)

Pause and Reflect

- In what areas of your life do you need to step out of your comfort zone?
- What hurts worse for you, discipline or regret?

Chapter 3

Pray For Closed Doors

Are you destined to take the path you're about to step onto? It might be worth the pause to ask that question.

When my husband and I were newly married, we learned the importance of praying for closed doors. It began as a simple prayer, asking God for guidance on a decision we were about to make regarding a vehicle purchase. As we were walking out the door to go to the dealership, I said, "Wait, we need to pray and make sure we are doing the right thing." We were new Christians, so we hadn't prayed out loud together before. Needless to say, the prayer wasn't very eloquent, but it was sincere. It went something like this:

"Dear Lord, We are getting ready to make a decision that we think is best, but if it is not, please close the door. We are looking to you for guidance. We love you, Lord, Amen."

At the time, we had an Eagle Talon that always drove perfectly and had never given us any problems, but as we pulled up into the dealership the engine stalled for a moment. We both agreed that was a weird anomaly but didn't think too much about it since it had never done that before.

After walking the lot with the car salesman, we decided on the car we wanted to purchase and were going through the paperwork process when the salesman asked if he could start the Eagle Talon we were going to trade in. As he turned the key in the ignition, it again did the same thing and stalled out. We were shocked and irritated since this was new to us and to make matters worse, it looked as if we were trying to trade in a lemon!

He gave us our keys back, and we got in our car to hopefully make it home. My husband put the keys in the ignition, and to our surprise, it started right up, and we drove home without a problem. In fact, the car never had that engine problem again! A month later, we understood why it occurred—a job change reduced our income, which would have made it impossible to manage the new car payment. God had answered our prayers and saved us from making a decision that would have made our lives much more difficult. We were so happy that He heard our prayer and closed the door on a decision that wasn't in our best interest.

Since that day, we have prayed that prayer many times, and God has always been faithful in answering it. It is such a simple prayer, but it accomplishes so much. We've learned that this prayer is not passive but takes active faith before it is answered. So many times when faced with making decisions or choosing between options, we don't know which path to take, so we freeze. We wait and we wait, hoping that God will audibly tell us what to do. We all know that it is impossible to steer a parked car, but if the car is moving, you can easily turn it left or right. The same is true with how God moves us. Once we take the first step of faith, He can easily direct us to our preferred destination.

If the destination you arrive at is not what you would have chosen, you can rest in the knowledge that it was for your own good. This all comes down to trust. Closed door prayers leave no room for disappointment. If you sincerely are seeking God's best for you, you won't be upset when He answers your prayer. You will understand that He knows what is best, and you will be thankful that He intervened in guiding your steps. When we ask God to close those doors for us, He is happy to do this as we are actively seeking His will.

If you've never done this before, I encourage you to test it out in your own life. Don't rush blindly after things you love or think you need. Hit pause, and ask God to direct your steps. You may just find that you avoided a bad relationship, tragic turn in the road, or poor financial decision.

Then the Lord said to Moses, "Why are you crying out to me? Tell the people to get moving!" (Exodus 14:15)

Pause and Reflect

- Can you rest in God's answer when He closes a door you would have preferred He opened?
- Reflect on a time where God's answer of *no* turned out to be a blessing in disguise. Thank Him for His sovereignty and for seeing around corners that you don't.

Chapter 4

His Divine Pattern

Throughout this book, you'll hear me offer advice from my own journey, and I hope it opens your eyes and heart to consider that no matter what you've been through, God knows and has a plan. We can't always see the fruit of our labor, or the rewards, but if you know God has given you a dream, keep going. Don't give up!

I started a ministry years ago that provides workout wear with a Christian message called Witness thru Fitness. The idea was inspired after I ran a marathon and realized the only things keeping my feet going were verses like Isaiah 40:31 and Philippians 4:13. I wanted to design shirts that would encourage both the recipient of the shirt as well as the reader. So that is what I did. I immediately started setting up at different marathons and health fairs. I was overjoyed that I was part of something that was furthering God's Kingdom in its own small way.

I was about to learn that everything worth doing has a price. It seemed that every high was followed by a low. In one of my weaker moments, I decided to take my store off-line and call it a day. I thought that God may be trying to tell me to stop what I was doing because if He was behind my endeavor, why was everything so hard? I took my site down, and not five minutes later, I received an email from someone that I had never met that read,

"Please put your store back online. You may never know how many lives you are touching through your shirts, but know that you are making a difference."

I was so excited to get this confirmation. God was working through my ministry!

Not long afterward, I ordered performance shirts. Cotton was not the material of choice for athletes, and I needed to invest in a more "breathable" fabric. I ordered boxes of t-shirts that said "Cross Training" on them with Matthew 16:24 underneath it ("If anyone would come after me, he must deny himself and take up his cross and follow me"). Money wasn't flowing for me, so purchasing these shirts was a step of faith.

When I received the shirts back from the printer, they looked great. I immediately started fulfilling orders. Again, I had a lot of joy and satisfaction knowing that God's word was going out into the world, even if it was on the back of a shirt.

Not long after, I started getting returns on all the shirts I sold. They were cut too small. What a nightmare! Instead of my shirts being a witness, they were sitting in a box in my closet, and I still had to pay for them!

I contacted the printer, and they said they had never had this problem and wanted me to come down and show them what I was talking about. As I was driving there, I prayed, "Why Lord? You know my heart. You know that I am doing this for You. I just want to be a good player on your team, but it seems like I keep getting benched. I just don't understand."

When I arrived at the printer, they looked at the shirts and agreed that they were indeed cut too small. They kept saying that they didn't understand how this could have happened. They used the same pattern that they always had, and none of the other shirts they produced were returned. Only mine. They wrote me a check for the shirts and even allowed me to keep them. I left the printer, happy that they refunded my money but still upset that the purpose of the shirts was unfulfilled.

Not long after this, I received an email from a ministry in Africa that sought to reach out to AIDS orphans and the youth in Africa through sports. They were requesting donations of soccer balls, basketballs, anything sports related. I was very hesitant because I had been scammed by a company in Africa that had purchased over $800 worth of shirts from me on a stolen credit card. I wasn't anxious to have this happen again. I deleted the email but as the day went on, I couldn't get this request off my mind. God impressed it upon my heart that I had a box full of singlets (a singlet is type of tank top that athletes wear) that were cut too small for my target audience but would be perfect for the youth in Africa. I agreed! I packed the box up and shipped it to Africa and was happy to do it.

After this incident, I put Witness thru Fitness on hold. I was weary of the battle and needed a break. However, Witness thru Fitness was always heavy on my heart. Like the request from Africa, it wouldn't go away. Through a series of events, I again put my store back online after a three-year hiatus, but this time, I wanted it to be more than selling shirts. I wanted it to include devotionals, testimonies, and the salvation message. God taught me through all that had happened that this was a ministry and not a business. So that is what I did, but things still weren't sailing as smoothly as I had anticipated.

After a particularly frustrating day, I was sitting at my computer and typed in "Witness thru Fitness" on a search engine. About four lines down on the results was a link from for a nonprofit organization called "Africa Youth Ministries." I clicked on the link, and to my delight, I saw a picture of a group of boys from Africa all wearing the shirts that I sent to them three years earlier! The caption under the picture said, "Thank you Witness Thru Fitness." I was overwhelmed with joy! All the frustration was wiped away when I knew there was a purpose in the pain.

God showed this to me at the perfect time to remind me that things aren't always what they seem. Just because I had frustrations didn't mean that what I was doing wasn't in His plan. He was behind the pattern when the shirts were being made. It was not a mistake that the shirts were cut too small. They were cut and designed perfectly for those boys, and a heavenly hand was behind it all. At the time, I focused on the problem and forgot God's promise that He works *all* things together for good for those who love Him and are called according to His purpose (Romans 8:28, emphasis added). I learned firsthand the reality of the Norman Vincent Peale quote that says that God's gifts to us are usually wrapped in a problem—the greater the problem, the greater the gift!

What a joy to be on His team. I now realize that I can rest, even when circumstances are not ideal, because I serve a God who not only runs the universe but the details of every aspect of my life and yours.

Why do we always have to feel as if we have to see confirmation of our success? Humans are wired this way, even when we are following God's plan. But consider this: God is a whole lot bigger and smarter than we are and is a supreme being, who orchestrates the big picture. What if we let go of the outcome of having to understand or justify what we believe God is doing? What if we couldn't possibly know? Whatever you've been through could have dramatically impacted or transformed someone else's life.

"For we live by faith, not by sight." (2 Corinthians 5:7)

Pause and Reflect

- In what areas of your life can you increase your faith by letting go and trusting God with the outcome?
- Blessings always follow obedience, but unlike the law of gravity, the law of reaping and sowing isn't always immediate. Be encouraged that God notices everything you do and promises to reward your obedience in His perfect time. Do you wait well?

Chapter 5

Choice Management

One of the primary reasons people say they cannot work out is a lack of time. The busyness of a career, supporting a family, and juggling the demands of life can be a challenge on their own. Time is necessary for everything in life: successful relationships, family bonding, creating a healthy lifestyle, or building a company. How can we make the right choices in life each and every day if we can't even make the right choice at lunch or dinner? It's tempting to reach for what's available and quick, rather than what's healthy and takes time. Each and every day we are presented with about a hundred different choices.

After signing up for my first full Ironman, I immediately began to worry about the intense training schedule that was involved in this new adventure. The thought of filling my already-packed day seemed more overwhelming than the race itself (2.4-mile swim, a 112-mile bike ride and a marathon 26.2-mile run, raced in that order and without a break). I immediately had buyer's remorse, and panic set in.

What I needed was a plan to add more hours to my day, a way to manage time. That's when I realized that time can't be managed—it is consistently and quickly slipping away from each of us at the same rate. A more accurate term would be choice management. I can't manage time, but I can manage the choices I make to fill the hours I have been given.

The Bible speaks of the importance of our time when it says, "Teach us to number our days, that we may present to You a heart of wisdom" (Psalm 90:12). I believe wise choices make the difference in merely living for today or living for eternity. So, before my training begins, I want to make sure that I keep things in the right order and not fall into the trap of worshiping the created over the Creator by not making time for the One who gave me the ability to engage in these activities in the first place.

If I am to be successful in this endeavor, then I need to consider my quiet time and Bible study as necessities that should be first on my choice management list for the day. Even professional athletes have to hire mental management coaches to help them compete and think better. Life isn't one-dimensional. We need to make time for all things.

I can't manage time but I can
manage the choices I make to
fill the hours I have been given.

This sounds wonderful as I am sitting here typing this, but I know that when fatigue sets in, the spirit is willing but the flesh is weak. I am not dependable when I think I can spend time with God later, I can read my Bible later, or I can be still later. Unfortunately, later is a dangerous word according to my daughter Skyler, who when she was three years old, was so exasperated at my responding to her many requests with "later" that she cried, "No, Mommy—later means never!" I guess she had some empirical data to back that statement up.

With that in mind, I should purpose in my heart to start my day with the One, who is the source of my strength. If I have the discipline to run marathons and train for an Ironman, then I certainly have enough discipline to put first things first. Jesus promises that if I seek first His kingdom and His righteousness, that all these things will be added (Matthew 6:33)—to include the time I need to train. For me, this is an important part of my life and my daily regimen. What's important to you?

I would encourage you to focus on all aspects of success—from physical fitness to mental fitness to spiritual fitness. What areas are you strong in? Make a list. At the same time, think of an area that requires more of your attention. If you feel unbalanced or longing for more in a specific area, whether it's physical, emotional, or spiritual, take steps to understand how to invest in that one area until you're strong.

"For physical training is of some value, but godliness has value for all things, holding promise for both the present life and the life to come." (1 Timothy 4:8)

Pause and Reflect

- What distractions are you allowing to steal your valuable time?
- Pray for God to give you a heart of wisdom so that you may learn to number your days. Ask Him to help prioritize your choice management list.

Chapter 6

The Bottom Shelf

Seventeen years ago, I decided that I wanted to learn how to sew, and I wanted my first project to be a king-sized quilt. I don't advise this approach to anyone wanting to try one's hand at quilt making because it was a whoopin'! Not only did I have to learn the basics of sewing (like threading the machine), but I had to learn how to cut and measure the fabric into small squares, then sew the squares together into long strips, then sew those strips together with the goal that it would form a nice pattern when it was all done. After the top part is complete, you have to get padding sewn in, and then it was my job to hand stitch all around the edges of a king-sized quilt. My little side project ended up taking me about three years to complete.

After I completed the quilt, I took a picture of it, then I folded it very carefully and put it on the top shelf in the cabinet, and that is where it stayed. I know the purpose of a blanket is to provide warmth and comfort to the user, but I was so worried that my kids would get hold of it and get it dirty that it was never used for its intended purpose.

Fast forward a few years later. I walked into my laundry room and saw my beloved quilt lying on the ground! I worried it that it might have gotten dust or dirt on it from being so intimate with the floor, but as I picked it up, I realized that there was more than dirt on my quilt. It was covered with grease stains on both the front and the back. It turns out, my husband made the mistake of using it to transport some work equipment in the back of our truck and when he was done, he threw it on the ground in the laundry room without realizing what blanket he used.

They say there are five stages of grief, and I think I went through all of them after this happened. My daughters remember me screaming and crying in the laundry room as I was going through the denial and anger stage—and this happened over a decade ago! When I finally got to the acceptance stage, I washed and dried it, then folded it up and put it on the bottom shelf of the cabinet. If someone wanted to use it, fine. What more could be done to it?

It turned out that this blanket became the favorite in our house. My girls always chose it when they had slumber parties (probably because it was so big). If people were visiting, they would choose the quilt to use, and even I, when I couldn't sleep at night, would always select it over every other blanket. Needless to say, it has been used a lot over the years, and because of that, it has been washed a lot. As I was folding it just the other day, I realized that over 98 percent of the stains that used to be there were gone! You see, every time it was put into service, it was washed. Every time it was washed, the stains were being broken down, the quilt was getting softer, and eventually the stains that I had thought destroyed my beloved blanket were almost nonexistent.

The story of my quilt applies to us as well. Why had I coveted it so much that I set it aside so that no one could use it? Looking back now, I am sure I had good intentions because I had worked so hard on it, but in the end, it was a better quilt because of its use, and I was better seeing it loved. That quilt kept so many people warm.

There are many people who don't want to risk getting involved in the messiness of life. They are afraid of getting dirty, or maybe they are afraid of getting hurt, so they stay high up on the shelf and never get to experience the joy of being utilized for their greater purpose.

Then there are those who have been hurt and stained by life. Unfortunately, they consider themselves damaged goods that bring nothing to the table. They falsely believe they have nothing to offer. So like the first group, but for a different reason, they stay on the top shelf. Some people hide their emotions or put security and safety over their desire to have more and do more.

The third group is stained and imperfect as well, but they stay on the bottom shelf, easily accessible and always available to love and serve others. Because of their wounds and their stains, they have great compassion for others. As they seek to serve, help, and comfort others, they find the blessing comes back to them, and slowly but surely their own wounds begin to heal. These are the servant leaders who understand that life is a patchwork quilt in itself, and no one is perfect.

You were created for a purpose. There is no amount of money, fame, or worldly success that is greater than the joy of doing what you were created to do. You have a gift that only you can give to a hurting world that needs what you have to offer. I promise that if you take the initiative, give what you can, serve where you can, and stay accessible by living on the bottom shelf, close to everyone else, you will never be disappointed in the Divine results. This requires strength—you have to be strong to step out in faith, and you are. You're a lot stronger than you think.

Your faith will become a Fantastic Adventure In Trusting Him.

"Dear children, let us not love with words or speech but with actions and in truth." (1 John 3:18)

Pause and Reflect

- What shelf are you on, the top shelf or bottom, and why?
- God never wastes our tears and will allow our miseries to be turned into ministries if we allow Him to. Where can you serve and give back because of your past, not in spite of it?

Chapter 7

Bloom Where You're Planted

It's easy to have faith when things go right, isn't it? When everything goes our way, it's pretty simple to say you've got faith, and you are trusting God to meet all your needs. But the true test comes when things don't really go the way you imagined.

Being a military wife for a number of years, I had to learn the importance of this quote early on. When my husband was in the Marine Corps, I had in mind the duty stations I thought were desirable and the ones that weren't. When I was told we were going to have to move on-base to a state that I had no desire to visit, let alone live in, I was a little bit of a baby about it. I wish I were exaggerating about the baby part, but I'm not. I cried when I found out, cried while driving there, and cried unpacking boxes in our tiny little base house in the middle of nowhere.

Then one morning about a week after we got there, I walked outside and noticed a sign in my neighbor's garden that said "Bloom where you are planted." It was then that I realized that I couldn't change my circumstance, but I could change my attitude. I was planted in this new location regardless of whether I liked it or not, so now it was up to me to decide if I were going to bloom and blossom or wither and wilt. I chose to bloom. I started meeting neighbors, I explored the neighborhood, I found a great job at an ad agency in town, and I quickly began to truly love and enjoy a duty station I never would have chosen. I am thankful that God sees around corners that we don't and, in His goodness, doesn't answer all prayers—to include the sincere, heartfelt ones. I look back now and realize the only duty station I cried going to was the only duty station I cried leaving!

Unfortunately, not all the wives took the advice of the "Bloom where you are planted" sign. There were some who were never happy where they were but were convinced if they could just hurry and get to a new duty station, they would be. I saw firsthand that this was never the case. They found out the saying, "wherever you go, there you are" is true. The problem is not the location or the circumstance but the attitude. No matter what situation you find yourself in, you have a choice to make—bloom or wither.

It has been said that the things you appreciate tend to get better, and the things you depreciate tend to get worse. When we stop focusing on the negative and start thanking God for everything, we discover that happiness is a byproduct of gratitude.

We've all seen bitter unhappy humans who complain about everything from the city they live in to the food they eat. What if we just made the decision to impact lives, be happy, and spread joy no matter where we traveled? Even if you moved to Alaska or Tonga from wherever you are now, chances are there would be someone there in need of the help that only you could provide. There's only one you, and the gifts inside you can change the lives of those around you.

The choice is yours—bloom or wither!

"Be anxious for nothing, but in everything, with prayer and supplication, with thanksgiving, let your requests be made know to God, then the peace of God which surpasses all understanding will guard your heart and mind in Christ Jesus." (Philippians 4:6)

Pause and Reflect

- Do you tend to focus on the positive or the negative?
- Think of a time when God didn't change your circumstance but instead changed you.

Chapter 8

Be a Seed Planter

How can you actively invest in the lives of others no matter where God takes you?

One of the greatest privileges we have as Christians is sharing the good news of the Gospel. When I say it is a privilege, it is. Think about it; Jesus is the one who was victorious at the cross, the one who suffered in order to redeem all who put their trust in Him, and yet He invites us to present to Him those He purchased through His blood. It's not unlike a parent who buys a present and allows the child to deliver it, and the child gets the credit!

What an amazing God we have and what an amazing privilege, but unfortunately, very few Christians actively share their faith. There are many reasons for this, I guess: fear of failure, fear of what others will think, overthinking it—and the list goes on. Hopefully, the following story about my garden will motivate you to seek the lost and become a joyful seed planter.

Years ago, I decided to try my hand at gardening, so my husband graciously got an area in our backyard ready, put a weed control layer down, made rows for me, and then entrusted me to do the planting. So I took my seed packet and was very careful about where I placed each seed—every seven inches, not any closer, not any further. As I was meticulously doing this, my daughter was bugging me to let her help. To keep her quiet, I gave her a packet of watermelon seeds and told her to plant them somewhere in the backyard but not in Mommy's garden. So she took her seeds and started flinging them all along the back fence area of our yard. She did it with joy and didn't fret over the placement, the location, or even the result. She just did what I told her to do.

Every day after that, we would go out and water the garden and nothing. Then one miraculous morning weeks later, right when I started to think I must have bought faulty seeds or there was "operator error" and I should give up on this gardening business, to my surprise, I saw little green plants sprouting. It was a miracle! I was so happy when I was watering my garden and amazed that all I had to do was plant this seed, and a plant was now growing. Then I looked over at the fence and saw an even greater miracle—a watermelon vine with watermelons everywhere was growing along the back fence! My daughter planted as many seeds as she could, and she was rewarded exceedingly, abundantly beyond all we could imagine!

I made a list of what I learned from this story.

Plant seeds! Lots of seeds. As many seeds as you can. I have had the joy of seeing many people come to faith in Christ, but the reason is not because I have been extra gifted in sharing the gospel; it is simply because I made the decision to tell as many people as I can, and then I allow God to take it from there. We don't have the power to make something grow, but we do have the power to plant.

Don't get discouraged if you don't see immediate results. Don't worry about the results when you are sharing the gospel. Just be obedient and leave the results up to God, knowing that He is the One who causes the growth. There are joy and blessings in obedience, and even if they refuse to receive what you are sharing, you will have peace in your heart doing the will of your Heavenly Father.

Planting seeds doesn't have to be as complicated as we make it. I have been asked how I share the gospel to a Muslim, a Hindu, or an atheist. My answer is, the same way you share the gospel to everyone else. The gospel doesn't change. God made it so simple that even a little child can understand it. "For God so loved the world that He gave His only Son, that whoever believes in Him shall not perish but have everlasting life" (John 3:16).

One day, we will get to rejoice in the fruits of our labor. What a glorious day that was for my daughter when she saw the multitudes of watermelons in our backyard all because she planted seeds. What an honor to be on God's gardening team and get to share in the joy of seeing multitudes of people in eternity because we were faithful in planting.

One of my favorite poems by Corrie Ten Boom says it best:

> When she gets to the beautiful city and the saved all
>   around her
> appear, many people will tell her, it was you who invited
>   me here!

Could there be anything better?

> "I planted, Apollos watered, but God was causing the growth."
> (1 Corinthians 3:6)

Pause and Reflect

- Have you missed opportunities by overthinking or waiting until you feel ready? Who can you share the gospel with today, trusting God with the results?

Chapter 9

Borrowed Belief

My heart raced as I stood in my wetsuit, surrounded by hundreds of other triathletes. This was my first official triathlon, and I was about to swim sixteen hundred meters, or a mile, in the open water. Not being the best swimmer, I told myself that I just needed to survive the swim and not worry about the waves, the other swimmers, my lack of experience, or my rapid pulse. In spite of my trepidations, I took courage from the prayers of my friend, Toni, who showed up that morning to support me. She reminded me that God would give me His strength, and she would be waiting at the shore for me.

It has been said that courage is not the absence of fear but the triumph over it. My choices were to give in and go home or get out there and try. I realized that quitting hurts worse than trying, so I started to make my way to the water. As I did, the road sign warning "Turn around, don't drown" was on auto-repeat in my brain. I was officially outside of my comfort zone. Doubts arose as my heart rate elevated and my pulse quickened. I shouldn't be this panicky, I thought, and I was second guessing my decision to do this when I remembered that you don't sign up for events like this if the goal is to be comfortable. If it were easy, then everyone would do it, so into the water I went.

I was able to swim along with the crowd for about five minutes on pure adrenaline, when suddenly it felt like my wetsuit was choking me. Panicking, I rolled over on my back so I could try and calm down. Big mistake. The choppy water crashed over my face, shooting lake water up my nose and giving me the sensation of drowning.

To make matters worse, I made the mistake of looking back to the shore and was reminded of how far out I was. I knew I didn't have the strength to swim back, let alone complete the rest of the swim course. I was drained of all energy and felt completely helpless.

Treading water, crying, and cussing myself for potentially being the first person in history to drown in a full, extra buoyant wetsuit, I looked up and saw the most beautiful sight—a woman on a kayak was paddling toward me, beckoning me to swim to the protective side of her boat. As I frantically splashed my way over, I prayed it wasn't a mirage.

"Are you okay?" she asked as I hung on for dear life to the side of her kayak. I was praying she would bring me back to the safe, dry land so I could be done with this ridiculousness. "No, I don't think so," my shaky voice replied, "I don't think I can do this." "Okay, how about you just swim to the next buoy, and then we will reevaluate? You are swimming great, and the next buoy isn't that far," she said as she pointed to the orange buoy ahead of us.

Reluctantly, I started to make my way to the next buoy, thinking that she was putting far too much faith in my swimming ability and couldn't possibly understand how dire my situation was—but as long as she stayed close to me, I would attempt the outrageous and continue to swim. My heart rate was so elevated that I could only swim about five strokes before I would have to stop, hold on to the kayak, cry, and continue to be strengthened by the words of this amazing woman who never once got irritated with me. She knew that I was struggling, so she chose to speak words of encouragement over me and spurred me on without any condemnation.

Since I was one of the last swimmers left in the lake, it didn't take long before another kayaker made his way toward me. Unfortunately, words of encouragement weren't his forte! In between my weak attempt at swimming five to ten strokes, followed by hanging on to the kayak, he (understandably) questioned me, "Did you even train for this?" To which my response was, "Swimming, yes; panic attack, no! It is kind of hard to train for that." At that point, he must have seen the fear in my eyes, so he tried to change the subject and asked if I had any hobbies. "Yes," I replied, "but open water swimming obviously isn't one of them."

I finally made it to the buoy where she had asked me to swim (thinking that my time in the water would be done) when she said, "You can quit, but look, the shore is right there. All you have to do it swim a little more. Look at how far you've come; you can easily do this!"

Miraculously, my friend on the kayak still had faith in me and seemed to really believe that I could make it to the shore. If I took her advice and kept swimming, maybe, just maybe, I could survive the swim! So I put my head down and prayed that God would loan me His strength just a little longer. Five minutes later and I was out of the water, and I had the joy of putting my feet on dry land, accomplishing something that I thought I couldn't do. The only one more excited than me to have completed the swim portion of the triathlon was Toni, who true to her word, was still waiting for me on the shore. "I knew you wouldn't quit!" she said with tears in her eyes. That statement alone made my decision to keep going, even in the midst of pain, more than worth it!

Lessons Learned

We need each other. Even though a triathlon is considered an individual sport, without encouragement from others, I wouldn't have been able to get past the first buoy. I could only go so far in my own strength, and when I thought I had reached that point, it was Toni's prayers as she waited on the shore and the encouraging words from the girl on the kayak that pushed me past my doubts. When I didn't believe in myself, I was able to borrow from their belief in me. It is so important to tell others that you believe in them, like the girl on the kayak did for me. Her words were extremely powerful because they lined up with her actions. She stayed by my side, was patient with me, and didn't waiver in her faith that I would make it to the shore. Her faith was contagious, and I began to believe right along with her. Instead of suffering the pain of defeat, I was able to experience the joy of victory!

"Therefore, encourage one another and build each other up."
(1 Thessalonians 5:11)

"And let us consider how we may spur one another on toward love and good deeds . . ." (Hebrews 10:24)

Just go from buoy to buoy. Like I said earlier, my first mistake occurred when I decided to stop and look back to the shore. My attitude wasn't, "Wow, look at how far I have come, but rather, look how far away I am." The great advice to just swim to the next buoy and then reevaluate forced me to look at my situation as doable as opposed to impossible. It seems human nature always assumes the worst when we look too far ahead, so focusing on the present really is a gift we give to ourselves.

"So do not worry about tomorrow; for tomorrow will care for itself. Each day has enough trouble of its own." (Matthew 6:34)

"Brothers, I do not consider that I have made it my own. But one thing I do: forgetting what lies behind and straining forward to what lies ahead." (Philippians 3:13)

Who are you going to listen to? I had two voices with me out there in the water: one that spoke words of encouragement ("You're swimming great . . . you're almost there . . ."), and one, maybe unknowingly, that spoke words that caused doubt ("Did you even train for this?"). I had to make a decision as to which voice I was going to listen to. There is power in the spoken word, and I was going to be the recipient of a prize that each awarded, based on which decision I made. Crying "uncle" and giving up offered the temporary reward of relief, but holding on and finishing what I started offered a lasting reward that can never be taken.

"The tongue has the power of life and death." (Proverbs 18:21)

"For our light and momentary troubles are achieving for us an eternal glory that far outweighs them all." (2 Corinthians 4:17)

It wasn't just about me. When I was struggling in the water and wanted to quit, I needed to remember that Toni was on the shore waiting for me. She was going through her own struggles that were far greater than mine. Her husband was in the last stages of battling a long fight with cancer, and he, along with Toni and Adam, their seven-year-old son, all got up early to support me. At one point, Adam looked up at his mom and said, "Do you think Jenny Mac drowned?" to which Toni reassured him that I didn't (she knew this because she had one of the boats come check on me!). "Well, do you think she is going to quit?" Toni told him "Jenny Mac will not quit."

When she told me this after the race, I was so relieved that I didn't! I had been encouraging her for so long to hold on, trust God, and just keep putting one foot in front of the other as Bill's cancer progressed. What if I had quit? She was crying in relief when I made it to the shore and kept saying, "I knew you wouldn't quit!" reminding me that what we do screams louder than anything we ever say. When the circumstances looked bleak and all seemed lost, my head finally popped out of the water, and to my surprise, I was finally on dry land. I know that was a visual that Toni needed to see. If He could get me safely to shore, there is nothing that He can't do!

As a side note, I am not condemning anyone who has quit at any stage during a race if they feel it is in their best interest. However, in my situation, it was evident to the volunteers that I had the ability to swim to the shore. I just needed to overcome the mental battle.

> *"Let your light so shine before men, that they may see your good works, and glorify your Father which is in heaven."* (Matthew 5:16)

> *"Jesus replied, 'What is impossible with man is possible with God.'"* (Luke 18:27)

Pain is a great teacher. Very rarely does someone have a great testimony without a test. The lessons I learned would not have happened had God not allowed me to struggle. Pain is a great teacher because, boy, how you learn! After finishing this triathlon, I knew I needed to practice swimming in the lake more and at the pool less. A wise swim coach once said, "The only way to get better at open water swimming is—open water swimming." I had already signed up for a full Ironman that was only four months away, so it was imperative that I practice, practice, practice! If failure is the tuition you pay for success, then I had given my down payment and was ready to get to the next level. What I needed to remember was that struggling is part of growing. God in His goodness, was teaching me that there is no such thing as a shortcut. If I were to improve, I needed to do my part, show up, and do the work. I took courage in knowing that, like the girl on the kayak who encouraged me and never left my side, God promises to do the same.

> *"Have I not commanded you? Be strong and courageous! Do not tremble or be dismayed, for the LORD your God is with you wherever you go."* (Joshua 1:9)

> *"Not only so, but we also glory in our sufferings, because we know that suffering produces perseverance; perseverance, character; and character, hope."* (Romans 5:3–4)

God never wastes our tears. I am so grateful for the help I received from the sweet volunteer that now I want to take kayak lessons! I want to volunteer just so I can pay her kindness forward. God showed me what it was like to feel afraid and panicky in the water, and because of that, I have compassion for others, who may experience the same thing. Like she did for me, I would love to inspire others to greatness by believing in them, encouraging them, and participating in the joy that comes from watching them succeed.

> *"Praise be to the God and Father of our Lord Jesus Christ, the Father of compassion and the God of all comfort, who comforts us in all our troubles, so that we can comfort those in any trouble with the comfort we ourselves receive from God."* (2 Corinthians 1:3–4)

* Four months later, I went on to complete my first full Ironman in Whistler, Canada. I pray that I will meet the girl on the kayak someday, so I can thank her, hug her, and let her know that it was because of her belief in me (that I had to borrow until it became my own) that made this victory possible.

I hope this motivates you to speak words of life over others, who are struggling. Who in your life can you "add courage to" as you encourage them with your words?

Pause and Reflect

- Think of someone who believed in you when you didn't believe in yourself. Send them a thank-you note to let them know how their words of encouragement helped you. Think of someone you can help.

Chapter 10

Get Up, Get Up, Get Up!

A while back, I participated in the Choose Life 5K that supported local pregnancy centers, including one where I am a counselor. Because of my affiliation with the center, I wanted to do my very best and place in my age category. All seemed to be going well until around the second mile, when I found myself flat on my face. I guess my right leg decided not to lift as high as it should have been, and I tripped and fell down hard. My good friend was right behind me, and she stopped, stood over me, and yelled, "Get up, get up, get up! You can cry at the finish line!"

Since she had never yelled at me before, the only thing I could do was get up, suck it up, and run. When I found out that I had placed and received a trophy, I realized the temporary pain of moving forward was well worth it. I credit her yelling at me when I needed it and not letting me stay down. The life lesson I learned was that we all need people who love us so much that they don't care if we get mad at them if their words and actions are in our best interest. I was so glad I got up, I was so glad someone made me get up, and I was so glad I didn't experience regret by quitting.

Fast forward a few years later, where I fell again, but this time it was on my bike. My husband and I were training for a triathlon, and we were just about to finish a successful seventy-mile ride. We were almost done, when it started to rain, making the road slick. As I was entering the parking lot, a mere 100 yards from my car, I turned too quickly, and my bike and I both went down hard. Now you have to understand how frustrating this was for me because I had just healed from the last time I fell on my bike only a week earlier. The pain, frustration, and fatigue kept me down, and I just lay there—in the middle of the parking lot, still clipped into my bike pedals, not wanting to move.

My husband stood over me and asked, "Are you going to get up?"

"I don't know," I answered. "Let me think about it for a second." As I lay there, I thought that maybe I needed to find a new hobby; maybe this just wasn't my thing. I mean, how many times did I have to fall before I realized this? Maybe God wanted me to be a spectator as opposed to a participant."

Have you ever spiraled downward into stinking thinking after a failure?

I don't know how long it took before I finally got up, but I imagine it must have been quite the sight. (Fortunately, when you are in the middle of a meltdown, you don't care about sideways glances, so I had that going for me). After what probably seemed like an eternity for my poor husband, I finally let him help me up. He wanted to take me home, so I could get my leg bandaged, but the pain in my stomach was worse than the pain in my leg so I said, "Let's get hamburgers at In–N-Out first. Then we can go home."

If you haven't been to an In-N-Out Burger, you may not know that they have scripture on their packaging. While wondering if I was a failure for falling, I looked at the bottom of my fries container, and it had Proverbs 24:16 printed on it. I looked the verse up, and it said, "For the righteous may fall seven times, and rises again..."

I was able to justify those fries for sure!

It was then that I realized that falling down doesn't make someone a failure; staying down does. What a personal God we serve that He would be concerned enough to remind me of this truth. After reading this, I had new resolve to keep trying, but more importantly, the fall in the parking lot probably saved my life only a week later on a training ride. I was going fast down a hill and about to turn around a corner on what is normally a quiet country road, when the memory of the previous week's fall (and the pain that followed), came to my mind. It was my nature to take this corner hard and fast, but as I began to pick up speed and make the turn, I remembered how that worked out for me the last time. I immediately slowed down and got behind my friend who was in front of me. At that exact moment, a car came flying around the corner. I came within inches of being hit by the speeding car, whose driver expected to see me as much as I expected to see him. Had I not slowed down and gotten over, I would have been hit. The moment took my breath away—another reminder of how quickly life can be taken. I'm thankful God used the memory of my previous fall to save my life.

Failure is a wonderful teacher as long as you learn from it! It is all about perspective. When you understand that failure is the first ingredient for success, you won't get discouraged. The only thing keeping us from our goals and desires is believing the lie that we can't get up, that we can't improve, and that we don't have what it takes.

When you understand that failure is the first ingredient for success, you won't get discouraged.

What it takes is persistence and a steadfast belief that our adequacy and our strength come from God. The Bible tells us that we can do *all* things through Christ who strengthens us. I believe persistence is more important than talent, education, and physical ability because it is the barometer of how much you want something and how many times you are willing to get up and try again until you succeed. It has been said that, "Hard work beats talent when talent doesn't work hard." Persistence is hard, but the rewards are more than worth it!

As for me, I am thankful I made the decision to get up and keep trying because only a few months later, I was able to successfully complete both a half and full Ironman and experience crossing the finish line where I could cry, but this time they were tears of joy!

"Blessed is the one who perseveres under trial because, having stood the test, that person will receive the crown of life that the Lord has promised to those who love him." (James 1:2)

Pause and Reflect

- Falling down hurts, but staying down hurts worse. Who can you encourage today to get up and keep moving?

Chapter 11

Thank God for Your Scars

Each one of us has scars if we live long enough, whether they're emotional or physical. Sometimes people have scars you just can't see, but they're bigger than the physical scars any of us have.

On October 29th, 2011, my sixteen-year-old daughter Savanna was driving to school for her cross country district meet. It was very early in the morning, still dark outside, with fog on the ground. Before she left, I hugged her and told her to text me as soon as she got there. I didn't like her driving in those conditions and prayed for her safety. If you ever had a kid just starting out driving, you know the panic that can set in.

Fifteen minutes later the phone rang. I picked it up and heard Savanna crying. She said, "Mom, I've been in an accident." I asked her if she was okay, and she replied, "Mom, there is a pole in my face."

I almost fell over in worry, not understanding how a pole could have hit her face. She then replied, "There is blood everywhere." My husband, Jason, heard me crying and grabbed the phone. He asked Savanna if there was anyone else there, and she said a man stopped to help. Jason spoke to him and frantically asked if Savanna was okay, but all the man could say was "I don't know."

The night before the accident, Savanna and her twelve-year-old little sister, Skyler, had been bickering and arguing over everything. In exasperation, I told them to hug each other and say, "I love you." Savanna did so without an argument (which is a miracle in itself), but Skyler refused. She said, "I am mad at her, and I won't do it." I reminded her that the Bible tells us not to let the sun go down on our anger. She wasn't willing to listen and went to her room to go to sleep for the night.

She woke up to me screaming that Savanna had been in an accident and that I didn't know if she was okay or not. She hit her knees and cried, "Mommy, I didn't tell her that I loved her. I refused, Mom!" What a painful lesson for a twelve year old to experience, but at the time, I couldn't respond to her.

When we got to the accident scene, it was worse than what we expected. Straight from a parent's nightmare—flares everywhere, firefighters, police cars, and an ambulance. That wasn't the worst of it. When we looked at Savanna's truck, it was almost too much to take. She had missed a sharp turn and struck a cattle fence. The force of the crash caused a steel pole from the fence to shoot like a rocket into the driver's side window of her truck. All her dad and I saw was the pole covered in blood. Even if she was alive, what could be left of her? The panic in my husband's eyes was evidence of the gravity of the situation.

I ran to the ambulance but didn't go in. I stood there afraid of what I would see when they opened the doors. Then I heard her say to the EMT, "Please get my Mom. "That was all it took, and I was by her side. Fortunately, they had her head wrapped but I could still see the damage to her nose and the blood that was all over her face. Even in her injured state, Savanna tried to make light of the situation by quoting a movie, "Don't worry Mom, it's merely a flesh wound . . ."

One of the emergency responders took a picture of Savanna's truck and gave it to her dad via cell phone. He said, "Sir, you were given a miracle. People do not walk away from accidents like this."

Jason and Skyler followed behind the ambulance as they rushed us to the Trauma Center in downtown Fort Worth. Jason said that it was a long ride, not knowing what was happening in the ambulance. Especially since they sped up halfway there and put their lights on. Savanna was complaining that her head was hurting, and they were worried that there was swelling of the brain.

After we got to the hospital, they rushed us in to have a CAT scan done to see if there was any internal damage. During this time, we were overwhelmed by the goodness of our friends and family, who came to be by our side. A lot of prayers were said for Savanna's safety and peace for us, as we waited on the results.

In the emergency room, Savanna had gotten a hold of her cell phone and was looking at herself in the camera after her bandages and wraps removed. The pole had hit her twice on her forehead and barely missed her left eye. You could see the circular form that it made from her eyebrow to her nose. She literally must have been looking down the middle of the steel pole. If it had hit anywhere else it would have taken her eyes out or killed her. Her nose was broken and would need many stitches to repair (her plastic surgeon says to this day she has never seen a nose that shattered). Her forehead cuts were so deep that you could see the muscle.

I told her to not look at herself right then because it is amazing what plastic surgeons can do these days. I couldn't imagine what was going through her mind—the girl, who freaked out over the occasional breakout, was now seeing her face after a horrific accident. She put her phone down, looked at me, and said, "Mom, I will never complain about my scars because God spared my eyes."

I was amazed at her answer and proud of her maturity. She told me that after the pole hit her, she couldn't see for a while because of all the blood and really believed she had lost her eyes or her vision. She had asked the first person on the scene if she still had her eyes, and all he could say was, "I don't know." What a relief when she found out that she didn't lose them. She was very grateful to God, and her scars were put into perspective. She was thankful that she could see her scars!

The CAT scan came back, and the results showed no swelling of the brain. We were so thankful! The plastic surgeon on call that particular day specialized in facial trauma—another blessing! While at the hospital, every nurse, doctor, and employee who saw Savanna said God must have big plans for her life because it was such a miracle that she was alive. Even in that frightening situation, God was getting glory, and we were thrilled about that. Only He can take something that was intended for harm and turn it into something good. Every parent's worst nightmare turned into a huge sense of relief and gratitude for our lives.

The surgery went well, and we were allowed to take her home after a couple of days. She had a lot of pain for a couple of weeks, but we planned on that. What we didn't plan on was how well she was healing (her dad kept calling her Wolverine!). I believe that when Savanna gave her heart over to God and His will for her life, not focusing on the scars but on His grace, that He said, "Here is another miracle for you!"

Her scars are barely noticeable now, but when I do see them, I am reminded of His mercy. Speaking of scars, the same God who healed her knows a thing or two about them. It's been said that Jesus' scars will be the only man-made thing in Heaven. A reminder for all of eternity of His immense love for us.

As far as Skyler goes, I was able to speak with her, regarding the accident. I reminded her that God spared her from a lifetime of pain when He chose to protect Savanna from an almost-fatal car accident. She would have had to live her whole life with regret. It was a difficult lesson to learn but one that will never be forgotten. She posted on her Facebook wall, "Tell your brothers, sisters, family and friends that you love them!"

I could not agree more. We are all just one phone call from our knees. Let's make the most of every day that we are given and choose to focus on the positive, being thankful for everything. Life is truly a gift.

"Do not let the sun go down while you are still angry..."
(Ephesians 4:26)

"Give thanks in all circumstances; for this is God's will for you in Christ Jesus." (1 Thessalonians 5:18)

Pause and Reflect

- Who in your life needs to be reminded that you love them? Who do you need to call? Who do you need to forgive?
- There is always something to be thankful for. Savanna didn't complain about her scars because she was so thankful she still had her vision to see them. It's all about perspective. In what areas of your life do you need to change what you focus on?

Chapter 12

Faith It 'til You Make It

What are some of your greatest lessons about faith? The thing that's interesting about faith is that we can't fully understand it or appreciate it until we let go. You have to let go of the need to control outcomes, let go of worry, and lean in to the life that God has to offer.

I learn something in every race I participate in, and the New Orleans Half Ironman was no exception. As I stood on the dock, waiting for my turn to jump into the angry waters of Lake Pontchartrain, I was silently having an argument with myself over whether or not I should take the plunge. I knew my ability as a swimmer was no match for the water waiting for me. I always tell my friends and family that fear is a feeling that will pass, so don't not do something just because fear is bullying you around. We miss out on so much by giving in to it. But in this case, I was reminded that God also gave me a brain, and I should use it. I didn't want to die for a tri! The weather conditions were horrible, with high winds whipping the waves into whitecaps, causing even seasoned triathletes to panic in the water. I didn't have faith in my ability to swim in conditions like this.

I was so torn because I realize you can't experience a miracle unless you "get out of the boat." The Bible tells us that Peter was able to miraculously walk on water with Jesus, but first he had to get past his fears and step out into the storm-tossed lake. Like Peter, I too would rather be a wet water walker over a dry boat talker! So I prayed for God to let me know what I should do. I was just minutes from having to decide before it was my turn to jump. I was just about to go against my own advice of giving in to fear when my friend, Veronica (who didn't know that I was silently freaking out), turned around, hugged me tight and said, "You're going to be okay."

"I am?"

"Yes."

And that was that. I knew what I was supposed to do—God would be with me, I was going to be okay, and I, like Peter, could get out of the boat. I chose not to worry about alligators, snakes, the occasional bull shark, panicked athletes, my ability, waves, or wind, and I bravely jumped into the water.

Now this is where Peter's story and mine differ. In the biblical account, Peter panicked after he got into the water (well, the moment he took His eyes off Jesus and instead focused on the storm). Jesus saw that He was sinking, took His hand, and said, "You of little faith, why did you doubt?" And then they climbed into the boat, and the wind died down.

I assumed that as soon as I jumped into the water, that God would say, "Peace, be still, Lake Pontchartrain!" But that didn't happen. It was actually worse than I thought it would be. Yet another lesson about faith: just because you let go, doesn't mean everything's going to be comfortable and smooth.

The waves crashed over my head, panicked triathletes were swimming over me to get to safety, and I couldn't see where the buoy that I was supposed to swim to was because the wind had blown it off course. I read about an eighty-year-old nun who does triathlons, and it's hard to imagine how someone in their ninth decade could have the fortitude to fight through that mess in the water.

The only thing I had going for me was, for the first time in my tri racing history, other people were struggling worse than I was! I thought, "Well, I am not that scared. I feel like this in almost every race." So I kept swimming because what else could I do? Sometimes as the inspirational fish Dory said in *Finding Nemo*, you gotta "just keep swimming" in life.

Once I made the decision to jump in, I knew I was going to stay the course and swim to that darn shoreline. After what seemed like an eternity, I finally made it to dry land. I don't know what I swam through, but I had black dirt all over my face (I like to think of it as war paint) and was told by one of the volunteers that I really should wash my face before I got onto my bike! It must have been bad, and I don't even want to know what it was.

I would love to say that the swim course was a test that I had passed, and the rest of the race was peaceful and still but that wasn't even close to being the case. Winds and heat make triathlons hard, and this day had both. It was almost comical how hard it was for me at times, but then I would think, "I didn't come this far just to come this far," and I would keep going. I had some solace in seeing that I wasn't the only one struggling. It was hard for everyone, so I wasn't alone in my pain.

After what felt like an eternity, I finally made it across that glorious finish line. I took my water, my medal, and my finisher's shirt and sat down, thinking about what had just happened. It was then that I realized that faith doesn't make things easy; it makes the impossible possible. I did what God wanted me to do, and He chose to allow me to struggle. I hurt the whole time, but the moment I crossed the finish line, none of that mattered. The joy of accomplishing this victory was worth the pain.

My faith in Him was strengthened because, even though it was hard, I knew He was there, pushing me the whole time. Would I have felt this feeling of accomplishment had I not had to fight for it? I knew I could not do this in my own strength. It took faith in His adequacy and not mine to get me into the water in the first place. Once I was in the water, I needed His strength to help me finish what I started.

The ironic thing is that I am always praying for strength and for God to increase my faith, but when He answers my prayer and sends me the very things needed to accomplish this, I get upset and question His training. I am very thankful of how patient God is. I am finally starting to realize that what is important is trusting His training plan because He knows what He is doing. I don't have to fake it until I make it. I just have to keep pushing and trust in Him.

So thank you, Lord, for the headwinds because they are making me stronger, thank you for the fear of jumping in the lake because it is an opportunity for my faith to increase, and thank you for my health and the ability to be able to participate in endurance events. I will continue to faith it 'til I make it!

> *"Such confidence we have through Christ toward God. Not that we are adequate in ourselves to consider anything as coming from ourselves, but our adequacy is from God."*
> (2 Corinthians 3:4–5)

Pause and Reflect

- Don't miss out on miracles by refusing "to get out of the boat." Think of an area where you are letting fear dominate, then purpose in your heart to face it head on. It is only then that you will understand that fear really is **F**alse **E**vidence **A**ppearing **R**eal.

Chapter 13

Train Your Brain

Anyone who's achieved massive goals in life, such as passing a test, raising a family, or some physical achievement, knows that it's important to train your mind and control your emotions. But what if you could train your brain to see stress as a positive fuel in life instead of an anxiety to be avoided? After completing my first Olympic triathlon, the next goal on my list was a half Ironman. Since I had empirical evidence that the swim portion of the triathlon was my weakness (the understatement of the year), I was terrified of having a repeat performance.

The night before the event, I was sitting at the dinner table with my husband, Jason, and some friends, who were participating as well. I was so nervous that I asked Jason not to even mention the race. It was then that my friend Christopher leaned over and asked why I was so stressed out. He went on to say very confidently that he loved that feeling. The racing of his heart, the jitters, the nerves, and the anxiety that occurs prior to races (or anything we do outside of our comfort zone, for that matter). I asked him "Why?" and he responded, "You can't manufacture this feeling in any other way but by actually getting in the game." Wow! He was feeling the exact same way I was, but instead of looking at it as a bad thing, he turned his anxiety around by embracing the pain and letting it work to his advantage. Where I was ruining my evening by worrying, he was giddy with excitement!

Since I wasn't about to give up and go home, I knew that I, like Christopher, would have to train my brain into believing that I loved this kind of stress. I wanted to welcome it because only the brave souls that show up and participate get to experience it.

Christopher's statement reminded me of a *TED Talks* broadcast that I had previously viewed on the subject of stress—and how to make it your friend by Kelly McGonigal. She spoke of how stress has been made into a public-health enemy, but new research suggests that stress may only be bad for you if you believe that to be the case. If you viewed your stress as a good thing—a sign your body was getting energized and preparing you to meet a challenge, then you could embrace it. That pounding heart is preparing you for action. If you're breathing faster, it's no problem. It's getting more oxygen to your brain. Those who have learned to view the stress response as helpful for their performance, well, they are less stressed out, less anxious, and more confident.

I wanted that confidence! I wanted to look forward to the race, and I wanted to use the stress that I was given (in abundance) to work for me and not against me. I visualized the race and as I did my heart started to pound—but—I purposefully changed my way of thinking and told myself that I loved it when my heart rate increased because my body was getting ready to rise up to a challenge. When I changed my thought process, my anxiety decreased. I was able to go back to the hotel room that night and not dread the next day. The power of our minds is amazing, and I am convinced that we need to include brain training to our workout schedule as much, if not more, than physical training. If we can't conquer the battle in the mind, how can we expect to get to the starting line?

Christopher's words helped me to get in the water the next day where I successfully finished my first half Ironman. Halfway through the swim portion, I started to experience what I previously thought was a panic attack, but then I remembered that this feeling is good, it's helping me conquer the swim, and it's working for me and not against me. That knowledge calmed me down, and I was able to keep swimming in spite of my racing heart.

My prayer for anyone reading this is to go outside your comfort zone, do hard things, and embrace the good stress that prepares you for greatness! Whether you think you *can* or you think you *can't*, you're right. Training your brain may involve a few extra steps than just understanding that it's important. Here are a few steps I've taken to master my emotions and train my brain to see stress as a fuel instead of something that takes me off focus.

Remember to be B.R.A.V.E.

I watched on online sermon entitled "BRAVE the Waves (Be anxious for nothing)" by Elevate Church that used this acronym to help when you are dealing with anxiety. It has helped me on more than one occasion, and I pray it helps you.

B—*Breathe*. That's it. Just breathe. When we are anxious, our breath tends to be rapid and shallow, encouraging our heart to beat even faster. So stop and breathe deep, calming breaths.

R—*Remember*. Remember what God has already brought you through. Repeat scripture back to Him and remind yourself of His promises. He promises to never leave you or forsake you. Remember this.

A—*Ask*. Ask God for what it is that you want. Present to Him your requests and wait expectantly for His answer, knowing that He is more than able to meet your needs.

V—*Visualize*. Visualize yourself accomplishing your request. See it in your mind. Remember that if you can see it through the eyes of faith, it belongs to you.

E—*Elevate*. You can elevate above your problem or fear by praising God. When we start praising Him in our storms, we are elevated above them and have a new perspective. Praise is warfare and forces our fears to flee. As we praise, we remember that God is bigger and stronger than any storm in our life.

"So do not fear, for I am with you; do not be dismayed, for I am your God. I will strengthen you and help you; I will uphold you with my righteous right hand." (Isaiah 41:10)

Pause and Reflect

- Stress can work for you if you harness it for good. Refuse to flee and worry and instead stand and fight. Face your challenge and then proceed as if success were inevitable.

Chapter 14

Are You Trying to Make Me Happy?

One of the hardest, yet most rewarding, New Year's resolutions I have made in the past was to purpose in my heart to assume the best before I assumed the worst in people. It sounded easy enough as I was penning it in my journal, but when I needed to apply it, it proved to be a bit more challenging. Like the boxer Mike Tyson has been quoted as saying, "Everyone has a plan—until they get hit!"

It seems as we get older, assuming the worst in others becomes the initial response. It is easier to go with "guilty until proven innocent" when you have been let down in the past because our defenses are up, and our faith in others is viewed through worst-case scenario glasses.

I guess God liked my resolution challenge because He didn't waste any time in providing me with a training ground to practice. I would like to say it happened with a stranger at a grocery store or something like that, but instead He chose an acquaintance at a Bible study! I was assigned to a small group, and I didn't know anyone in my class. As I was looking around at all the new faces, I was thrilled to see a familiar one walk into the room. It was a woman I had met before through mutual friends. I was excited she was assigned to my group!

Unfortunately, I found out rather quickly that the feeling wasn't mutual. My smiles and attempts at conversation with her were met with one-word answers and quick exits after our study was over. My initial response was the one I had been practicing for quite some time, and that was to assume the worst. However, I had a resolution that I was trying to keep, and I was going to "do hard things" and assume that she was just shy. Years before this happened, I had a friend who I thought was stuck up and rude, but it turned out that wasn't the case at all. She was a humble and sweet girl who was just extremely shy and had trouble speaking in group settings. With this memory in mind, I assumed that my friend in Bible study had this same fear.

Six months went by, and I continued to greet her and smile when I saw her in class. I started to feel genuine compassion for someone who was so shy! It wasn't until she pulled me aside one night and said, "I need to talk to you." I was thrilled; she was finally talking to me. I killed her with kindness, and now she was coming out of her shell. Then she surprised me with, "I have never liked you."

I wasn't sure what the correct response to that was so I just stood there as she continued, "but God has convicted my heart, and I realize I may have lost out on what could have been a good friend. Would you please forgive me?"

I was floored. My first thought was "I knew it!" But then I realized if I would have acted on this fact, the story would have ended differently. Because I chose to practice my resolution, I didn't have to lose one night of sleep over someone who disliked me for no reason but instead spent that time having compassion for her. God did what only He can do and fought this battle for me. He was the one who convicted her heart and helped her apologize to me. Even though I was correct in my initial assessment of the situation, I did myself a favor by overriding that and focusing on the best. I saved myself from bitterness, resentment, and most likely a fight with a fellow Christian who needed Jesus to deal with her and not me. It was to my benefit to not take the situation as personal—even though it was directed at me. As for her, I am thankful that she had the courage to apologize, and because of her actions, we are now friends.

Assuming the best is not easy, and I don't think it will ever be second nature for me. It's a decision that I have to be intentional about every day, but the good news is that I have plenty of opportunities to practice! My goal is to be like my daughter, Skyler, who, years ago, demonstrated a very nonconfrontational way of communicating without automatically assuming the worst in someone.

She was about four years old, sitting in her car seat when her dad went faster than she would have liked over a dip in the road. Her older sisters loved it when he did this, but I guess Skyler didn't. She didn't want to hurt her dad's feelings if he was doing it for her sake, so she simply said, "Daddy, are you trying to make me happy?" Before he got a chance to answer she continued with, "Because you're not." She went on to say that she didn't like that yucky feeling in her tummy when he went fast even though her sisters did.

I love how she didn't immediately get defensive but instead assumed that her Daddy was only trying to make her happy. We have used this phrase many a times in our household when faced with the choice of assumption. "Are you trying to make me happy? Because you are!" Or, "Are you trying to make me happy? Because you're not!"

As a side note, assuming the best doesn't mean being naive; it is simply choosing not to attend every argument your mind invites you to. If someone has bad intentions, God will deal with them while at the same time carrying a burden that only He is strong enough to carry. That should make all of us happy!

> "Who will bring any charge against those whom God has chosen? It is God who justifies. Who then is the one who condemns? No one. Christ Jesus who died—more than that, who was raised to life—is at the right hand of God and is also interceding for us." (Romans 8:33)

Pause and Reflect

- You give yourself the gift of peace when you choose to assume the best in others as opposed to assuming the worst. Can you trust God to deal with the difficult people in your life?

Chapter 15

Pick Your Perspective

Have you ever been in a situation that brought you pain when it should have brought you joy? Was it the circumstance itself or how you were viewing it? It's amazing how much power our attitudes have over our emotions. It is even more amazing how much power our emotions have over us if we allow them to go unchecked.

When I ran my first marathon, the entire goal was simply to finish. I remember the joy I felt when I finally reached the finish line because I had accomplished the impossible. I had just traveled 26.2 miles, and I wasn't in a car! I was on cloud nine as the race volunteers placed my medal around my neck. Every part of my body hurt, but it didn't matter because I was an official marathon runner. In my euphoric state, I started contemplating what other impossible feats I could tackle. If I could run 26.2 miles without dying, there was nothing I couldn't do. What mountains could I climb? What oceans could I cross? What world problems could I solve? The high was so great that I knew I wouldn't be a "one and done" marathon runner. I had already started thinking of the next race I would enter.

Unfortunately, it only took a few more marathons before I realized I had to up the ante in order to duplicate that former feeling of accomplishment. I knew I could finish a marathon, so now it became all about getting faster and setting PRs (personal records), so I joined a local running group in order to get properly trained.

It wasn't long before I learned about the Boston Marathon. In order to register for this prestigious race, you have to qualify. I was so excited about this new goal. If I could just run fast enough, I would have the honor of becoming not just an average marathon runner but a *Boston Marathon* runner. All I needed to do was finish in under three hours and forty five minutes (for my gender and age), and I could participate. My friend Toni wanted the same honor, so we set out on this journey together. It was during this time that I realized that sometimes the things that make a person great can also become their greatest weakness.

For example, a competitive nature can spur you on to achieve great things, but it can also steal hard-earned joy if you allow it to. I found this out the hard way when Toni qualified for the Boston Marathon before I did. I wanted to go to Boston with her, so I signed up for five marathons in one year in order to try and qualify. Instead of getting faster, I was getting slower at each race, and instead of rejoicing in the accomplishment of completing the grueling task of running 26.2 miles, I was crying over not being "good enough." Sorrow and resentment started to creep in and I became a distraught mess. Running wasn't fun anymore.

I think I finally hit runner's rock bottom when in my final chance to qualify for the 2012 Boston Marathon, Toni decided to help by running with me, and you guessed it, she qualified again and I didn't.

Now don't get me wrong, I was very happy for Toni, but deep in my heart, I wondered why God kept inviting her to this "party" and not me. Why was I being excluded? Why couldn't He just loan me His strength for a measly three hours and forty five minutes of one day! I was disappointed in myself and sad, and to make matters worse, I was mad that I was sad! Certainly there were far greater problems in the world than my desire to qualify for the Boston Marathon.

After this marathon, I was walking to my car, holding a medal that I didn't even look at because in my mind, it represented failure.

That was my final chance to qualify for the 2012 Boston Marathon, and I didn't even come close to qualifying. I was crying as I walked to my car when I got a text from a friend that said, "Faith in God also includes having faith in His timing."

How amazing that God impressed it upon her heart to send me that text right when I needed to hear it. My emotions had clouded my vision for so long, God knew I needed to be reminded that He is in charge of every detail of my life, including timing. In the meantime, I needed to embrace the fact that I was enrolled in a "wait training" class, and I didn't get to pick when it ended. I did pray that I would be a good student so that I could advance quickly. (I wanted patience—now!) I wanted the faith needed to advance and did not want to be like the Israelites of the Old Testament, who had to wander around the desert for forty years because of disbelief. Fortunately, I didn't have to wait that long.

The following October, Toni and I were about to begin the St. George Marathon in Utah when she asked, "Do you believe you can qualify for Boston?" I told her that I had already proven time and time again that I couldn't qualify in my own strength, but if God wanted to loan me His, I could. Either way, whether I qualified or not, I purposed in my heart to not focus on a number but rather enjoy the journey and be grateful that I had the ability to run 26.2 miles! I wanted to enjoy running again without putting pressure on myself to perform.

Lo and behold, when I took the focus off of performance and instead chose to be grateful for every step I took, I took twenty minutes off my previous time and qualified for the Boston Marathon with five minutes to spare! I trained the same way as I had previously; the only difference was what I chose to focus on.

When I chose to "look up," giving God the glory and understanding that my strength, joy, satisfaction, worth, and ability comes from Him alone, I had peace in my heart. I didn't have to perform to make Him happy or proud; He already was. He gave me the desire to run and the enemy of my soul wanted to take that away, and I almost let him. Through all of this I learned the importance of picking my perspective. I realized that my previous failed attempts at qualifying were actually a gift. It wasn't until I was fully aware of my weakness that I finally allowed God to be strong in my life. He wanted to give me the desire of my heart but not until my heart was right. He knows when we are ready to handle the gifts He has in store for us. Our job is to trust our Trainer, trust His timing, trust His plan for us is good, and trust in His strength alone to get us to the finish line. The greater the struggle, the greater the reward because we serve a God who never wastes our tears!

So what are you focusing on? Are your circumstances happening to you or for you?

"Lead me in Your truth and teach me,
For You are the God of my salvation;
For You I wait all the day.
(Psalm 25:5)

Pause and Reflect

- How much power are you allowing your emotions to have over you?
- Worry ends where faith in God begins because one cancels the other out. Live the abundant life by choosing faith and trusting God's perfect timing. Make the conscience choice to look up.

Chapter 16

Can You See?

Focus is important if we want to succeed in life. I'm sure you've had one of those days where you felt like you were going nonstop, spinning your wheels, and accomplishing nothing. When we are distracted, multitasking and not focusing, we are like a dim flashlight that can barely light a room. However, if we can focus, we are more like a laser beam—so powerful it can cut through steel. In light of this, we need to be intentional about what we see and make sure we are focusing on what is important.

I was almost a mile into the swim portion of a triathlon, struggling against rolling waves that were so bad I was actually feeling seasick. All I could do at this point was endure and pray that I could get to the shore before I threw up. I couldn't help but think that I paid good money for this torture and wondered if I secretly hated myself. As I was swimming, I felt something hit me on my foot, not once but twice. I looked up to see a volunteer on a kayak who was shouting at me. He told me to stop and hold on to his kayak then he said, "Can you see?"

I didn't respond right away because I was wondering how bad I must have been swimming for him to ask me this question, when he continued, "The shore is that way," as he pointed to the right, "and you are swimming to the left. You're going the wrong way."

I have a tendency to swim to the left on a good day, and with the waves encouraging my already bad habit, he was right—I was way off course. The funny thing is that I thought I was swimming straight and would have kept on going if he hadn't taken the time to stop me and show me the way. I'm so thankful he pointed me in the right direction.

When I finally made it, I ran to the transition area and started the bike portion of the triathlon. About halfway in, I came to an intersection where some athletes were turning right and some were going straight. I missed the sign telling me where I should go, and I was kicking myself for not looking over the map like my husband said I should do before a race. I asked a volunteer if I needed to go straight or turn. He very confidently pointed for me to keep going straight, so that's what I did. After the bike portion was over, I finished up the run and was very grateful to finally be done with this hard-fought battle.

Later that evening, I was looking at my race results online and saw that I came in fourth place in my age division. My excitement only lasted a moment when I realized why. According to the results, I was riding twenty-five mph on my bike, and I knew that was not the case! The only way this could have happened was if I missed a turn—which I now realized I did. The volunteer I asked directions from was sincere, but he was sincerely wrong when he told me to go straight. Once I realized what happened, I emailed the race director and let him know, so instead of placing, I was disqualified. Needless to say, I learned many lessons from this experience that can be applied to the Christian life.

The first lesson was to be sure and always read the road map before the start of a race. My husband was right when he said it was important in order to know where I was going. How much more so for us to know what the ultimate road map, God's word, says! In His goodness, God gave us the gift of the Bible that includes directions on how to navigate through life, but we have to read it for it be useful. The Bible says it is a lamp to our feet and a light to our path (Psalm 119:105). We don't need to wander in the darkness, miss turns, or go in the wrong direction when we are given a map that shows us where to go.

The second takeaway from this educational day was how the kayaker was intentional and determined to help me. He saw that I was off course and did what he had to do to get my attention. He must have been yelling at me for a while before he finally had to hit me with his paddle! I'm glad he was persistent and didn't give up until he knew that I saw and heard him. He did his part, and then it was up to me to listen and obey his good advice.

As Christians, we should be like the kayaker and be determined and intentional in seeking the spiritually lost and pointing them in the right direction. There are hurting people in this world who desperately need to hear the good news of the Gospel. I love my friend Tammy's mission statement for her life. She told me she intends to stand at the gates of hell and redirect traffic. She understands that all of us, at one time or another, were spiritually lost until someone got our attention and directed us to Jesus.

I have to say, it's a relief to know that it is not our responsibility to convince others, but like the man on the kayak, we are to simply tell the truth. He didn't jump into the water and force me to swim to the safety of the shore; that wasn't his job. He got my attention, warned me that I was going the wrong way, and then told me what I needed to do. That is all that is required of us. I believe it is one of the greatest privileges of being a child of God, and yet so many fail to take part in the Great Commission. I can't encourage you enough to share the gospel because if you don't, your voice will be replaced by a world that is even more intentional, more determined, and more vigilant to keep people lost and as far away from God as possible.

During my race, it seemed the pattern for the day was getting off track. One person gave me good information, and the other unknowingly gave me bad info that led me straight to a DQ (disqualification). As sad as I was that this happened, it was just a triathlon and not the end of the world. But spiritually speaking, I can't think of anything more tragic than to find out you are disqualified from entering into a beautiful eternity because you listened and acted upon bad advice. Proverbs 14:12 tells us that there is a way that appears to be right, but in the end it leads to death. Again, that is why we need to study our road map.

Jesus is the only One who can qualify us. We have all broke God's laws, and Jesus took the punishment we deserve upon Himself. He paid a fine we could never pay on the cross so that God the Father can dismiss our case (see Isaiah 53). Our part is to acknowledge our need for Him, repent of our sins, and ask Him to save us. If you choose to run the race of this life and feel you have no need for Jesus, you will one day find that you are eternally disqualified and lost forever. I promise you aren't holy enough, strong enough, fast enough, good enough, or wise enough to make it to the podium. If you trust in yourself and your abilities, a DQ is all you will earn.

Like the kayaker, I want to seek the lost. Like my friend, I want to redirect steps and point others in the right direction. I encourage you to allow the One, who has already won the race, to be your qualifier.

* * *

After the Boston Marathon I began to realize that it's not just the miracles there that matter but the ones in everyday life. You've likely seen miracles in your own life, and they may have been small but significant. When I speak at organizations, a lot of times they ask me to talk about my experience at Boston, but I always try to talk about the small miracles in life that can change your own journey or impact someone else. He is both the God of our eternity and the God of our moments. I can't encourage you enough to focus on what is important and shine in this dark world for the One who has opened our eyes.

"So we fix our eyes not on what is seen, but on what is unseen, since what is seen is temporary, but what is unseen is eternal." (2 Corinthians 4:18)

Pause and Reflect

- Who in your life is "swimming" the wrong way and needs to be redirected?
- Have you been sincerely wrong about someone or something in your life? Let this memory make you realize how important reading God's word is to keep you on course and out of danger.

Chapter 17

Look People in the Eye

How many times have we rushed through our day, even when we are serving others in our own families or at church, but forgotten to slow down and make eye contact and make them feel loved and appreciated?

One of my very good friends, Cyndi Bunch, runs a nonprofit ministry called Phillip's Wish. It is a wonderful organization started by her son when he was only seven years old. Little Phillip's heart hurt over all the people he saw on the streets of Fort Worth one winter and was worried that they were cold. Unlike many adults, he decided to take it upon himself and do something about it. So with the faith of a child, he emptied his piggy bank and told his mom that he wanted to make sure everyone he saw outside would be warm. He gave his mom the change from his piggy bank—all he had—and asked her to buy a blanket with it. Needless to say, what started out as a child stepping out in faith by confronting a problem most people would turn away from, one blanket turned into thousands, and within a year a ministry to serve the homeless was born.

I had the privilege of meeting Cyndi on a cold December evening, the day after little Phillip's request. She was standing on a street corner in downtown Fort Worth handing out flyers that simply asked for blanket donations. I was more than happy to help her; in fact, meeting her was an answered prayer for me. I had prayed the night before for God to put an opportunity in my path where I could teach my girls what Christmas was all about. I wanted them to see firsthand that it was more about giving, serving, and loving and less about expensive toys on a Christmas list. God heard my prayer and as I was walking downtown, Cyndi startled me by literally walking right onto my path!

It turns out I was the first one to call her back the next day and take her up on her simple request. As a side note, it's always best if you can be the first to help someone because when you do, you will always have a special place in their heart and will never be forgotten. I am so fortunate to have been the first to help Cyndi because we have been friends ever since, and yes, my girls got to see up close and personal the importance and privilege of helping others and the confirmation of Jesus' words when He said it is far better to give than receive.

I could write hundreds of stories based on what I have learned and experienced while helping Cyndi and Phillip serve the homeless. Little Phillip's actions are a testament of what stepping out in faith can do, no matter how old you are or how little you have to give. In fact, one of the most powerful lessons I've learned while helping Cyndi is how important just showing up is. Sometimes all that matters is our presence.

I was handing out blankets with Phillip's Wish one winter when I was approached by a homeless man in his early twenties. Figuring he wanted one, I tried handing him a blanket, which he politely turned down. "No, thank you," he said, "I already have one. I was just wondering is if you knew where I could use the bathroom."

I wasn't expecting his question, and I had no idea what to tell him. He continued by pointing across the street to the overnight shelter that had a line wrapped around it. He explained that there was no way he could get a room that evening, and since he couldn't get a room, where was he supposed to use the bathroom?

I didn't have an answer, so we both stood there for a second looking at each other—it was one of those rare moments where I was at a loss for words. I finally told him I was so sorry I couldn't help, and I truly meant it. He brought tears to my eyes when he said, "Oh, but you have helped me—more than you know. You looked at me."

With that he walked away, and as he did I began to recall all the times I had seen the homeless on the streets and averted my eyes because I didn't want to deal with an uncomfortable situation. I told my husband about had happened, and he pointed out how blessed we are that things that man lacked were basic needs that we take for granted every day.

Each of us has a desire to "know and be known." We are all relational beings, and whether we admit it or not, we need each other. Since the man that I met began living on the streets, he was introduced to a society that, like I had previously done, chose not to look at him. He wasn't asking me for money; he just wanted someone to acknowledge him. He needed to be reminded that he wasn't invisible and that he mattered. The homeless have the same needs as you and me. They have a need for significance, to know that they matter and are not ignored.

Since that day, when I speak on behalf of Phillip's Wish, I try to always remind the volunteers that minister to the homeless to take the time and interact with those they meet, stopping to look them in the eyes, listen to their stories, and pray for them. By doing this, you are showing them that they are loved and not forgotten.

We don't need a lot of money to help others, and we don't need to have all the answers to solve the problem of homelessness. What we do need is to show up. I promise, they long for your presence as much, if not more, than your presents. To quote another homeless man I met that same day, "When faith, love, and action meet—it is a powerful thing."

"Dear children, let us not love with words or speech but with actions and in truth." (1 John 3:18)

Pause and Reflect

- We all have a desire to know and be known. Even the simplest act of smiling at a stranger is letting them know that you see them, you acknowledge them, and that they matter. Purpose to connect with others by taking the time to look people in the eye and smile! Not only will you bless them, but their return smile will bless you.

Chapter 18

Don't You Quit 'til You Get Your Miracle!

At the beginning of every New Year, I pray for one word that is personal between God and me. The word is usually something that He is trying to perfect in me, something that I need to be reminded of, or something that I need to practice. Rarely do I get the same word for two years in a row, but when my word was endure, I did (I am just now seeing the irony in this as I type). If ever I wanted to be a quick learner, it was during the "endure" years. I had many different issues that I could expand on—relational, financial, and so forth, but I am going to focus on my triathlon training. I know that sounds like a first-world problem, but the lessons learned are applicable to every issue I faced during this time.

As you already know by reading the previous chapters, I was not a quick learner when it came to the swim portion of the tri, but I was determined! The first thing I did was ask a swim coach, who had experience in endurance events, to help me. Not only did she have experience, but she was the best. I always find it funny when people who don't know much about marathons or triathlons ask me if "I won." I wish I could say, "Yes, yes, I did. I came in first place in the marathon," but that is just a social fantasy. My friend Shanna, however, can answer this question in the affirmative because she does win almost every endurance event she enters! I figured I would start at the top because I needed all the help I could get.

The first day I met her for open-water training, my husband and I were already in the lake when she showed up, and I was attempting to keep up with him. He is a great swimmer, and even on my best day, that would be an impossible feat. However, on this particular day, keeping up with him was the least of my problems. Not drowning was more of an issue! I had never swum with a wetsuit on before, and I had the feeling of being suffocated because it felt so tight around my neck. I lay on my back and called for Jason to help me. He quickly swam to my side, held on to me for few minutes to calm me down, and then started swimming me to the shore. When we finally arrived, Shanna said that my swimming looked great and followed with, "You guys must really love each other, hugging in the middle of swim practice and all." I had to laugh when I realized what it must have looked like from her perspective on the shore. I told her, I do love Jason, but that wasn't why I was hugging him. I was actually hanging on to him for dear life!

She laughed and gave me a few pointers that would help me. After my first performance, I knew I needed more than a few! As I stood in the shallow end of the lake, I realized the extent of the predicament I was in. I (before even doing a sprint tri) signed up for a full Ironman event that was only a few months out, so I had to figure this out; quitting could not be an option. The problem was, at that very moment, I could not see how that would be possible.

At about that time, a group of three others showed up, got into the water, and started swimming effortlessly. I wanted to be able to do what they were doing and wondered if their parents had put them on the swim team when they were two or something. As they were exiting the lake, they had to walk past me, and that was when I told them how jealous I was of their abilities. I was shocked when one of them told me that it hasn't always been easy. She went on to tell me how she really struggled with the swim portion of triathlons, and on her first race, she cried the whole time she was swimming because it was so hard. As she crossed the finish line after biking and running, she was still crying. Her husband asked her why, and she said "because of the stupid swim!"

Wow! How could the person, whom I just witnessed swimming beautifully, have ever struggled the way she did? I needed to hear this; we all need hope to cope, and her story gave me a sparkle of just that—hope. As she was encouraging me to keep at it, her friend spoke up and said very confidently, "Don't you quit 'til you get your miracle."

Don't you quit 'til you get your miracle.

What a profound statement! God knew that I would need this reminder for the season I was about to enter, and I had to call on it many, many times. When I wanted to give up, when things felt too hard or too scary or too overwhelming, I would remind myself that I hadn't received my miracle yet, and until I did, I would not quit— as tempting as it was. I needed to remember that it usually takes years of practice, failures, discipline, and heartache to become an overnight success! My new friends, who were good at swimming, didn't start out swimming effortlessly, but they ended up that way because they, too, didn't quit.

Perseverance, endurance, steadfastness, and discipline are what made them so lucky. I needed to embrace this mindset, not only for swimming but also for the other areas in my life that were in need of miraculous intervention. I needed to patiently do my part and wait for God's perfect timing for my breakthrough. That is so hard for most of us because we never know when the breakthrough will come. We have faith in God but not faith in His timing. It seems He is never in a hurry to answer our very urgent prayer requests. I needed to remember that His timing is perfect, and because I have a limited perspective, mine isn't. This is where it gets hard and trust becomes vital.

After I was told not to quit until I got my miracle, it brought back a memory of something that happened years earlier when I wanted my kids to go to a private Christian school but didn't have the funds to make my dream a reality. I started praying with my daughters that God would provide a way. In the meantime, I proceeded as if success were inevitable and purchased them school uniforms and went through all the necessary steps to get them enrolled. Every time we would be in our car and see a sticker on the back of a vehicle with that particular school's logo, we would pray that God would hold a place for the girls and give us a miracle. We did this all summer in the hope that they could attend in the fall.

I began to panic the night before I had to give the school a down payment for them to hold a spot, and I still didn't have the financial ability to make this happen. My prayer hadn't been answered, and I didn't have a Plan B. I walked into my youngest daughter's room to kiss her goodnight when she asked, "Mommy, did we get our miracle yet?"

My heart sunk as I told her, "No." She didn't seemed phased at all, kissed me goodnight, and proceeded to fall into a peaceful sleep, not worried about a thing. As I walked out of her room, I realized she wasn't worried about whether the prayer would be answered; she was just asking about the when. She truly believed God had every intention of answering our prayer when she finished her sentence with the word *yet*.

Oh to have faith like a child! I repented of my unbelief, and the very next day, I found out that the school was hiring for a position I was qualified for. I sent my application in and ended up getting the job! For years after that, I thanked God every day for not only giving us our miracle but going above and beyond and allowing me to go to school with them. That is the exceedingly, abundantly part of all that we ask or can even imagine when we take our requests before the God of the universe. If we can see it through the eyes of faith, it belongs to us!

With this memory now fresh in my mind, I realized God knew the exact words that would motivate me to push through the pain and help me endure until I got my miracle. I can't tell you how many times I had to repeat this in my head as I struggled with the doubt and unbelief that bullies its way into my mind when pain is present.

Endure was definitely an appropriate word for me, and endure I did. In fact, I endured to the point of getting my miracle! It took almost two years of suffering through the swim portions of triathlons before I finally had my breakthrough. Up until that time, it seemed I wasn't progressing at all and struggled in every race I entered. What I didn't realize then was that progress is still progress even if it is slow. Every time I showed up and did hard things, I was in training. I didn't realize it at the time, but I was getting stronger, braver, and better at swimming by refusing to quit.

Fast forward to my second full Ironman. As I stood on the shore, waiting for my turn to enter the water, I anticipated the pain that was to come until the swim portion was over. Can you imagine my overwhelming joy when I got into the water, started swimming, and felt great? My breathing was controlled, I wasn't panicking in spite of getting hit, kicked, and swum over (I had experienced this before in previous triathlons and survived every time, so I knew I was fine), and miracle on top of miracle, I was enjoying the swim! When I got to the finish, I looked at my watch and wanted to cry happy tears when I saw that I had taken off over thirty minutes from my previous Ironman swim. I was overjoyed, and now I am a believer in the power of perseverance.

When we step out in faith in spite of our fears, it loses its power over us. When it loses its power, we are free to start living in the miracle zone—our thinking changes and instead of "I can't do that," it becomes "I can do all things through Christ who strengthens me." Jesus takes us from strength to strength, and the more we obediently follow Him, in spite of our fears, the more our faith grows. Then we are allowed to participate in an adventure that the faint of heart can only be able to observe from the sidelines.

Don't quit until you get your miracle!

"For everything that was written in the past was written to teach us, so that through the endurance taught in the Scriptures and the encouragement they provide we might have hope." (Romans 15:4)

Pause and Reflect

- Pray for God to give you a word for the year and then put it on your refrigerator so that you can be reminded every day of what He wants to perfect in you.
- Refuse to sit on the sidelines of life. Choose to get in the game even if it is scary. I promise you, the feeling of accomplishing the impossible is indescribable as God moves you from strength to strength. Choose to dream big and never give up!

Chapter 19

Where Do You Run?

Years ago I read a story of a hunter who was surprised by a frightened bunny that frantically jumped out of the bushes and ran straight toward him, seeking shelter between his legs. As he was puzzling over this, the story became a bit clearer when a few seconds later another character entered the scene. Out of the same bushes that delivered the bunny came a hungry weasel, which wasn't happy to see his potential lunch sitting at the feet of a man with a gun. The weasel froze in its tracks as he stared at the hunter. The hunter looked down at the rabbit, still squeezed between his hunting boots, heart racing, and completely spent, and realized that the poor thing must have run as fast as it could and was close to death before running to him as its last source of refuge.

The hunter didn't disappoint the defenseless rabbit as he raised his gun and shot at the ground sending the weasel scurrying away in fear.

"Where did he go, little one?" the man tenderly asked the frightened rabbit. "Where did he go?"

I think of this story every time I make the mistake of not running to God first. Like the rabbit, we too have an enemy who would love to destroy us. The Bible says that the devil roams around like a roaring lion, seeking someone to devour (1 Peter 5:8). In our own strength, we would be defenseless, but if we belong to Jesus and run to Him for protection, we realize the enemy is only able to roar.

My friend's three-year-old daughter, Sydney, said it best when she told her mom, "the devil is loud, and worry is pretend." She then went on to say, "If you know God, you never have to worry, but if you don't know God, then you do. The devil is very loud and scary, but God isn't. He is quiet so you have to listen."

Wow—out of the mouths of babes! I love when she said that worry is pretend. When we are scared or sad or lonely, don't we always imagine worst-case scenarios and create pretend scenes in our minds of things that will probably never happen? Mark Twain once said, "I've lived through many tragedies in my life, some of which have actually occurred."

Do you feel that the predator of worry is about to overtake you? Where will you run when your past pursues you? Where will you run when temptation is pounding on the door? Where will you run when your fear feels stronger than your faith? What will you do when your energy is spent and all seems lost? I pray that from this moment on, you will immediately run to your Savior—not as a last resort but as your first reaction.

Remember that He is your protector, your hiding place, and your victory. In the light of His presence, darkness has no choice but to flee. Yes, we are weak, but He is strong, and through Him, we are more than conquerors! When you draw near to God, you can boldly tell the enemy to pound sand and send that predator scurrying away in fear!

"Submit yourselves, then, to God. Resist the devil, and he will flee from you. Come near to God and he will come near to you." (James 4:7–8)

"God is our refuge and strength, a very present help in trouble." (Psalm 46–1)

"You are my hiding place; you preserve me from trouble; you surround me with songs of deliverance." (Psalm 32:7)

Pause and Reflect

- Do you run to your Heavenly Father as your first resort, or is He your last resort? When you are worried, scared, stressed, etc., do you call a friend or family member first or do you take it immediately to the Lord?

Chapter 20

Actively Waiting

Have you ever waited for something for what seemed like forever?

One of my favorite verses in the Bible is Matthew 7:7—"Ask and it will be given to you; seek and you will find; knock and the door will be opened to you." I love this because God is giving us permission to present our requests before Him. If what we want lines up with His perfect will, we can be confident that our prayers will be answered. I have no problem presenting my requests before God because I know that whatever His answer is will be in my best interest. I love to pray, "Lord, I really would like it if (fill in the blank), but if you say "No," that is okay—but please don't let it be that I didn't ask."

God has answered many of my prayers with "yes." He has answered many of my prayers with "no," and He has answered many of my prayers with "not yet." I am okay with all of the above because I trust that He sees around corners that I don't, and He wants what is best for me. It has been said that if we could see the whole picture, God's will would always be our will!

So what do you do if you think the answer is "not yet"? The verse says for us to ask, seek, and knock. We all want our prayers answered in the first stage, but sometimes we have to go beyond just asking and start seeking and knocking as well. I call this actively waiting for my prayer request.

When my request was to overcome my fear of open-water swimming, I would have loved it if my prayer were instantly answered and I could miraculously swim like a pro overnight—but that's not how it worked. I believed God wanted to answer my prayer, but I knew I had a part to play as well. I actively waited by seeking instruction and knocking at the pool or lake's door four or five times a week to practice swimming. I was proving by my actions how badly I wanted this prayer answered. What I may have believed was a "no" if I stopped at the asking stage was a "yes" all along, but I had to go through the training. When my prayer was answered, not only did my faith grow, but my strength and endurance did as well.

If you are actively waiting for something, I encourage you to trust the process, enjoy the journey, be consistent and persistent, and actively wait for His perfect timing.

Then He said to them, "Suppose one of you has a friend, and goes to him at midnight and says to him, 'Friend, lend me three loaves; for a friend of mine has come to me from a journey, and I have nothing to set before him'; and from inside he answers and says, 'Do not bother me; the door has already been shut and my children and I are in bed; I cannot get up and give you anything.' "I tell you, even though he will not get up and give him anything because he is his friend, yet because of his persistence he will get up and give him as much as he needs. (Luke 11:5–10)

Yet those who wait for the Lord
Will gain new strength;
They will mount up with wings like eagles,
They will run and not get tired,
They will walk and not become weary.
(Isaiah 40:31)

Pause and Reflect

- Make a list of areas where you are waiting on the Lord. Are you *actively* waiting by praying, being obedient, and trusting His guidance? Is there anything He is asking you to do during the waiting process?

Chapter 21

Lean In

The words of the missionary William Carey have always motivated me to step out of my comfort zone when I read his call to arms to "Expect great things from God and attempt great things for God."

We honor God when we trust Him completely and depend on His adequacy to accomplish great things. Think about when you are asking a child, who can't swim, to jump into your arms in the pool. How does it make you feel when he or she doesn't trust you and refuses to take the plunge? It's even worse when it is your own child. Even though they don't know how to swim, you are more than able to catch them and carry them above their fears and limitations. It's not their strength but yours they should depend on. It hurts to think your child is not confident in your ability to catch them but instead chooses to focus only on their inability.

Counter that scenario with the child who confidently jumps into the deep end, knowing you will catch them. It is a great compliment to be trusted. That brave child is putting their very life into your hands and depending on your ability alone, and the reward is great! Even though the child can't swim, he is splashing around in the deep end, head above the water, and experiencing something exciting, something that couldn't have happened without you carrying him.

Now think of Peter walking on the waves with Jesus. He must have been beside himself with excitement as he was experiencing the impossible and living in the miracle zone. Everything was fine until he took his eyes off the one who was able to make Him stand and instead focused on his limited abilities. The miracle of walking on water was so easy for Jesus to accomplish that he said to Peter, as he was pulling him up, "you of little faith, why did you doubt?" If it just takes a little faith in Jesus to walk on water, then what miracles can be accomplished with great faith?

I want to live like that. I want to expect great things from God as I attempt great things for God. I want to get out of the boat and walk on water. I want to jump into the deep end, confident that God will always catch me, and I want to encourage as many people as I can to do the same. The best thing about living life in complete surrender and confidence in God alone is that He will be the one who gets the glory, while at the same time our faith will be strengthened and our love for Him will grow. There is great intimacy with those we trust.

My favorite definition for faith is simply confidence in God. He invites us to lean into Him and be empowered by His Holy Spirit. That may be hard for some people to understand, but go with me here as I use an analogy regarding my dog. Our Doberman, Jett, loves to lean into certain people. We always know if she likes someone because she will stand right next to them and lean in with all her weight—to the point where she would probably fall over if they were to walk away too quickly! It's her doggy way of hugging someone, I guess. I tell those chosen few who get this treatment that it is a compliment because I've never seen her lean into someone she didn't love and trust.

God is waiting for you to lean in to Him as you trust that He will hold you up with His everlasting arms. Our Redeemer is strong, and He never tires. Only He can carry those who trust in Him not only today but forever! Psalm 28:8-9 is a great reminder: "The LORD is their strength, And He is a saving defense to His anointed. Save Your people and bless Your inheritance; Be their shepherd also, and carry them forever."

"The eternal God is thy Refuge, and underneath are the everlasting arms." (Deuteronomy 33:37)

Pause and Reflect

- What great thing can you attempt for God?
- We honor God when we trust Him in spite of our doubts. How you can you honor Him with your life today?

Chapter 22

The Power of We

As I wrote this book and the thoughts came flooding forward, I realized that if there's just one thing you learn or takeaway from this journey here, it's been worth the read. It's a daunting task to create a book, and the responsibility of coming up with the right words and putting them in the right order is something that requires persistence and patience and courage. Whether you come away from this with a reminder to trust God or renewed perseverance or faith in yourself, I trust that you'll be stronger because iron sharpens iron. It's been a wonderful journey to take with you, and I'm honored you've come this far.

Have you ever found it hard to accept help from others and even harder to admit your need for it? We sometimes try and fix our problems like a two-year-old, who repeatedly says, "I can do it myself," not realizing we are missing out on a gift that is ours for the taking, while at the same time, robbing others of the joy that comes from helping. We all know deep in our hearts that it's greater to give than to receive, so why do we try to refuse a gift when it is offered to us?

I was at mile eighty of a hundred-mile bike ride when I found myself in a bad place. The wind had picked up, my legs were screaming, and my attitude was not, shall we say, positive. I was hurting both physically and mentally. My problems started when instead of riding my own race, I tried to keep up with Jason—

which I couldn't do. Fortunately, we had made plans to meet at every other water stop if we got separated. This worked out well for him because he usually had about ten minutes to rest, eat, and recover before I would show up. Worried that I was holding him back, I didn't take advantage of any of those things. I would let him know that I was okay and ready to go. I just kept pushing through, running on empty.

Not taking in nutrition while on your bike works as well as driving a car without gas. When the external forces of wind and hills at mile eighty entered the scene, it was almost too much for me to handle. To make matters worse, during this particular stretch of the road, I was by myself. Jason had once again gotten ahead of me, and I was all alone in my pain. "Please God, give me a second wind," I prayed. If He chose not to answer this prayer, Plan B was calling Uber or a taxi—like I said, I was in a bad place!

Right after I prayed this, seemingly out of nowhere, a group of three bike riders pulled up beside me. The woman leading the group said, "Hi, how are you doing?"

I was surprised at their sudden appearance and replied, "I've been better. How are you?"

"Great" she answered, and before I knew it she pulled ahead with the two other riders behind her, leaving me at the back of their mini peloton. For the first time in my riding life I got to experience the feeling of drafting (drafting is a trick where cyclists will go in single file to block the wind for the other people behind them, and take turns being the one in front). The sweet lady who greeted me was currently in the lead and doing the hard work. Since I was at the back, it felt like I was being pulled along. She maintained the lead for about fifteen minutes, then when she got tired, she then moved to the back as the next person did the hard work for a while.

This continued until everyone took a turn as the lead cyclist, and before I knew it I was at the next water stop and thanking God for answering my prayer and teaching me a valuable lesson. You see, when I asked God for a second wind, I was just asking for my strength to increase as I rode solo. Instead, He sent in a team, and we all worked together. Being surrounded by them, my energy was renewed, and because the work was divided, I had the strength to continue this strenuous undertaking. Before they showed up, I was isolated, throwing a pity party, and ready to quit.

God speaks to us in what we know, and during this ride, He taught me the importance of community. When life is hard, the worst thing we can do is isolate ourselves. Whether we feel like it or not, we should surround ourselves with strong, encouraging friends who can help when our struggles are too heavy to carry alone. A magnet I read years ago says it best, "a joy shared is twice as great, and a burden shared is half as heavy."

We have been created in the image of God and since God is relational, so are we. The Bible confirms this in Genesis 2:18 when it says, "It is not good for man to be alone." Think about it—all of our best and worst memories are attached to someone, which means we are relational to the core. Besides being relational, when we are together, we are powerful. I am convinced one of the reasons the enemy of our soul wants to isolate people is because he knows that when we are united, there is nothing that we can't accomplish. If you are a visual learner, then imagine an ember in the fireplace, isolated and alone. It is not very effective and in a very short period of time, it will burn out. But what happens when all the embers are close to each other and united? A raging fire is produced, and the more kindling that is added, the stronger the fire becomes. It's like spiritual thermodynamics: "the greater the heat, the greater the expansion!"

There is power in numbers, and when you are gathered with fellow believers, you are granted supernatural power! Jesus told us that "If two of you on earth agree about anything you ask for, it will be done for you by my Father in heaven. For where two or three come together in my name, there I am with them" (Matthew 18:19–20). That was spoken in the New Testament, but did you know that God also said that in the Old Testament as well? In Genesis 11:6 we read, "The Lord said, 'If as one people speaking the same language they have begun to do this, then nothing they plan to do will be impossible for them.'"

The people at the time did not have good intentions, so God confused their language and scattered them, but the principle of the power of unity is clear. If unbelieving, corrupt individuals can accomplish the impossible when working together, how much more power do we as God's children, filled with His Holy Spirit, have? With 100 percent confidence, I can say that we can do even greater things than Jesus did while He walked the earth. How can I be so confident? Because He was the one who said it: "I tell you the truth, anyone who has faith in me will do what I have been doing. He will do even greater things than these, because I am going to the Father" (John 14:12).

Knowing this, we should be diligent to stay close to our fellow believers, guard against division, get out there, and change the world! We can do all things through Christ who strengthens us (Philippians 4:13), so let's light up this dark world and shine bright as we speak and act through the power of the Holy Spirit. Together, nothing will be impossible!

"Trust in the Lord with all your heart and do not lean on your
own understanding.
In all your ways acknowledge Him, and He will make your
paths straight." (Proverbs 3:5–6)

Pause and Reflect

- Are you part of a Bible study or a group of fellow believers? If not, get involved, believing that together you can shine brighter than you can alone. Together you will make a huge difference in this dark word.
- Do you agree that a burden shared is half as heavy? Pray for God to direct you to someone who needs a helping hand.

Chapter 23

Fight Forward

Have you ever been in a fight and felt like giving up? I'm not talking about a literal fight, but a fight for your peace of mind, or an inner struggle that challenged you. When this happens, we need others to lift us up and support us along the way. There are times when we need someone to inspire us, tell us to keep moving, or help us see a different point of view. We need each other in this world even when we don't understand this type of "help" at the time.

The saying, "You don't get what you want, you get what you fight for" was all I could think of as I made the decision to flip over on my back and start swimming toward my goal. I was halfway through my first half Ironman swim, and I was determined to not make the mistake of stopping and treading water when I got tired. No matter what happened, I purposed in my heart that I would continue to keep forward momentum. I didn't care how much it hurt; I was going to fight forward!

It's amazing the things we can accomplish when we are properly motivated. For me, my motivation was a shirt—the Buffalo Springs Ironman shirt—to be exact. I received it the night before at packet pickup and was so excited that I made the rookie move of putting it on and wearing it to dinner that evening. As I sat down, I noticed a "look" on my friend's face.

"What? I asked. When she didn't reply right away, I said, "Am I not supposed to wear this shirt?"

"Well there isn't an official rule saying you can't," she replied. "It's more like an unspoken one, but you shouldn't wear the Ironman shirt until you complete the event."

I was feeling both embarrassed and irritated as I walked back to my hotel room to change my shirt. What a stupid, unspoken rule that is, I thought. Who was going to see me anyway? What I didn't realize at the time, was this conversation was good for me because it became my tackling fuel for the next day's events.

When I needed motivation to keep going, I just had to think about that shirt, unwearable forbidden fruit, unless I finished! I would get a surge of adrenaline every time I remembered what I was fighting for. By making the choice to fight forward, continually moving in the direction of my goal, I was able to wear my shirt with a big smile that evening as we all celebrated our victories at dinner.

Learning how to fight forward is crucial if we are to be successful in this world. We are all faced with challenges, battles, problems, and situations that try to keep us from our dreams and will stop us in our tracks if we allow them to. Maybe you are prone to paralysis by analysis by overthinking, which causes you to do nothing but think. Or you may be waiting on God, standing still as you cry to Him for direction so you can make your next move. Either way, you're not going in the direction you want because you're not moving!

Even when we are waiting on God, we should be preparing to receive what He wants to give us. I learned this early on, when as a new Christian, I read the verse in the Bible that says to always be prepared to give an answer to everyone who asks you to give the reason for the hope that you have (1 Peter 3:15). I realized that if I wanted to share the gospel, I needed to start memorizing verses, so I would be ready. I began on Monday and every day for a week, I memorized keys verses in Romans that would help me to explain the gospel clearly. On Friday, not ten minutes after I had memorized the final verse I intended to, my phone rang. It was the pastor from my church who told me I had a neighbor who lived a few doors down who communicated through a comment card that she wanted to know more about Jesus, and he wanted me to share the gospel with her! Whoa! I took God seriously, and as I prepared and sought His wisdom, He took me seriously and put me into service. Prepare your fields; then be prepared to receive a great harvest in God's perfect timing.

Successful people are people of action. God is the one who leads us and guides us, but He requires us to start walking in faith so He can easily direct us. Faith is active! Our faith precedes the miracle—it is the vehicle that drives us there. Engagement brings clarity, and as you make decisions and act, the path you are on gets brighter and brighter. I promise, you will arrive at your dream, but it will be one step at a time! Will it be hard? Yes. Will you want to quit? Yes. In fact, you can be assured you are on the right road if you feel like you are climbing a mountain. If you are coasting, you are going downhill, and that does not build the strength and endurance you need to be successful. Besides, has anything worth doing ever been easy?

Trust the dream that God has given you and, starting now, prepare to receive help along the way, dig deep, find your motivation, and fight forward!

"The path of the righteous is like the morning sun, shining ever brighter till the full light of day." (Proverbs 4:18)

"It shall be done to you according to your faith." (Matthew 9:29)

Pause and Reflect

- What motivates you?
- Ask God what His dream is for your life is and then start moving in that direction, one step at a time.

Chapter 24

It Doesn't Belong to You

Humans have a desire for significance built into us. It's because you yourself were created in the image of God. What could drive us to be more significant than that? Without even knowing it, we desire significance, to be worthy, to matter because God matters. You are significant, and your life can make a significant difference to others.

I read a Facebook meme recently that said, "When you taste significance, success will never again satisfy you." I couldn't agree more. I wrote this book, knowing that my life experiences will allow me to give back to others through words for generations.

When I get to the end of my life, I want to have peace, knowing that I chose to put people over possessions, significance over success, and memories over money. I want to live a life that matters and leave a legacy that points to Jesus. I don't believe there is anything wrong with being successful. God wants to bless us so that we can be a blessing to others (the Good Samaritan had more than good intentions; he also had money that paid to help the injured man. See Luke 10:25–37). Our problems arise when success is defined by temporary, material possessions. Why? Because it will never be enough to satisfy our soul. The world's definition of success is an illusion that keeps us chasing after the wind.

I recently attended a John Maxwell conference where Nick Vujicic, who was born with no arms or legs, was a speaker. I was frantically taking notes as he spoke because he had so many nuggets of wisdom, but one of my favorites was, "If you put your happiness in temporary things, your happiness will be temporary." He articulated what I am trying to say in one sentence!

My friend Tammy Kling had the opportunity to introduce Nick to her best friend, a gorgeous girl with long dark flowing hair, and they now have two children. He sure is being blessed with a lot of amazing things here on earth but still, to this day, puts his faith in eternal things by living his life's calling. Nick has to travel all over the world to fulfil his calling and leave his family at long stretches—a huge sacrifice. But he does it anyway. Make sacrifices and finish the race strong, even if you don't know why you're doing it sometimes! God will show you the way.

The good news is that if we chase significance first, success will follow. This type of success won't drag along the sorrows that selfish ambition brings. Jesus confirms this in Matthew 6:33 when He said that if we seek first His kingdom and His righteousness, all these things will be given to us as well. There is great joy when we are successful and able to be generous on every occasion. God promises to supply all of our needs, and that includes giving. The day I grasped the truth that God owns everything and I was just a steward of His possessions, tithing and giving became a *get to* and not a *have to*. I love being a conduit for His blessings because He has an endless supply. I never want to be like a stopped-up sink, where the faucet needs to be turned off because water is not flowing. I want the faucet to be on full blast.

Recently, I was reminded again of why having purpose and pursuing significance is more important than worldly success. After years of volunteering as a counselor at a pregnancy center, I put it on hold so I could work full-time. I wasn't happy after a few months in spite of my paycheck and the awesome benefits that came with my new job. I had tasted significance for over twelve years at the pregnancy center, and during that time my definition of success had changed. When I was there, I was doing what God had called me to do, and when I gave that up, no amount of money or status could fill that void.

It was a conversation with my friend Lidia that confirmed that my days at the center were not done. I told her I wasn't volunteering at the moment to which she replied, "You have to. You have to share your story with the girls. You have to go back, and you have to help them. If not you, then who?" She was so intentional and emotional when she spoke, it felt like I was getting marching orders from an angel! She really believed what I did there was important.

I wish I could say I immediately listened to her advice, but I was still hesitant. I didn't want to throw away a good job if that was where I was supposed to be. A few weeks after that, my husband and I were sitting in church when a man walked over to us, turned to Jason, and said, "Thank you for sharing your story at our men's group a few months ago. It really encouraged me." I told him how nice it was of him to take the time to say thank you. He smiled at me and replied, "Our testimonies don't belong to us."

And that was that. Unless God put a billboard on the side of the road that said, "Jennifer, go back to the pregnancy center," He couldn't have made it anymore clear. I finally listened and found that my good job was keeping me from my great purpose.

Our testimonies don't belong to us, our stories don't belong to us, and if we want God to use our tears for good, we need to be willing to share our lives with others. The Bible states that "God comforts us in our troubles so that we can comfort others" (2 Corinthians 1:4). Let's remember to chase after Him first so that He can bless us beyond what we can imagine not only in this life but in the one to come.

"It is the blessing of the LORD that makes rich, and He adds no sorrow to it." (Proverbs 10:22)

"But seek first His kingdom and His righteousness, and all these things will be added to you." (Matthew 6:33)

Pause and Reflect

- Never be ashamed of your story, but share it to help others. Your testimony doesn't belong to you, so use it to help a lost and hurting world. If not you, then who?

Chapter 25

Unfinished Business

There is nothing more unsettling for me than to start something I can't finish. I'm built to finish strong, and honestly, I know we all are. Finish the race strong. God put this desire in you. The stubborn side of me knows that beginnings are easy, but the challenge is finishing—because that's where strength and grit have to overrule the temporary relief of quitting. I think this is where I get the discipline to finish the endurance events I participate in. I know that if I start, unless I physically can't, I will not quit until I get to the finish line. I don't want to give in and feel regret later. I want to be an example for my kids and teach them that anything worth doing is going to require a sacrifice. I believe it is the sacrifice that gives it worth.

There is a story in the Bible that illustrates this perfectly. In 2nd Samuel 24:24, King David was told that he didn't have to purchase the land he wanted to buy, but rather, it would be given to him. He responded by saying, "No, but I will surely buy it from you for a price, for I will not offer burnt offerings to the LORD my God which cost me nothing." It costs something to finish what you start.

For many years my unfinished business was completing my four-year degree. I was in my junior year at the University of Nevada-Reno when I married Jason. He graduated one year ahead of me with military orders to report to Quantico, Virginia. He was a newly commissioned officer in the Marine Corps, who had received a coveted flight slot. He was fulfilling his dream to be a pilot with the ultimate goal of flying jets. I gladly went with him as we reported to his new duty station, thinking I could finish my degree any time.

It's amazing how quickly life goes by. Before I knew it, years had passed, and my dream of crossing the college graduate finish line seemed out of reach. For a while I gave up on it and convinced myself I didn't need to finish everything I started. For example, I didn't need to finish every argument with the last word or finish a bad movie just because I started watching it (you can't get those two hours of your life back). So I pretended that I didn't care about getting my bachelor's degree—but I did. It's hard to fool yourself. No matter what your dreams are, don't forget that they're your own. No one else can dream your dreams for you. Your dreams are placed in your heart by God. Every dream matters, and nothing is too foolish.

In a previous chapter entitled "Fight Forward," I said I was able to accomplish a goal because I was properly motivated. In that incident, it was a shirt; in this one, it was a box, not a physical box but the box you have to check on forms that ask if you graduated from college or not. I would get frustrated because that little, tiny, small box didn't have enough room for me to explain why I wasn't able to graduate. I felt the need to say that I was so close! I was almost there! I have three years under my belt and two years of community college; does that count?

Now don't get me wrong, I don't believe everyone needs a college degree, and I didn't believe getting a degree would make me more valuable in God's or my family's eyes. I was just bothered that I started something that I didn't finish. To make matters worse, I thought this dream couldn't happen because I let too much time pass, and besides, it would be silly for me to be a college student at the age of forty. Then one day I read an Earl Nightingale quote that jumped off the screen at me. It said, "Don't let the fear of the time it will take to accomplish something stand in the way of your doing it. The time will pass anyway; we might just as well put that passing time to the best possible use."

That was the nudge I needed to start walking toward the impossible goal of finishing college, and a few months later, I was enrolled at the University of Texas at Arlington. It's amazing how quickly life goes by. In what seemed like a blink of an eye, I graduated cum laude with a Bachelor of Arts in Communication Technology and a minor in English. I was able to able to not only cross this finish line, but this time around, I was able to finish well. Desire realized truly is sweet to the soul!

If you are reading this and you feel like you don't have enough time, resources, or motivation to finish what you started, let my story encourage you to not make excuses anymore. You owe it, not only to yourself, but to all those who are watching you. I love hearing from others who tell me they were inspired to go back to school after seeing that I did. In fact, I love hearing that even more than being able to make big checkmarks on the little boxes asking if I am a college graduate or not.

Remember, success isn't just about what you accomplish but also what you inspire others to do.

"The end of a matter is better than its beginning, and patience is better than pride." (Ecclesiastes 7:8)

Pause and Reflect

- Refuse to make excuses for the unfinished business in your life. Remind yourself that if you are good at making excuses, then that is the only thing you will be good at. Do it now, do it now, do it now!

Chapter 26

Be All There

Have you ever had a wakeup call that caused you to see yourself in a new light? I'm sharing my failures and observations here because they've caused me to grow. How many times have we lectured to our kids and then gone and done the exact same thing we lectured them about?

I went to a Pinterest craft fair recently and found the line to enter was long and slow. In frustration, I pulled out my phone, so I could enter my own little virtual world. I must have stood there for over twenty minutes, but it went by quickly because I was busy liking Facebook posts, reading emails, and responding to texts. It really is amazing how technology has enabled us to connect with others anywhere in the world at any time—something that couldn't even be imagined in previous generations. Time and distance are not factors anymore, making our small world even smaller. We are connected to each other like never before.

Or are we?

That evening I was reading the local news on my phone and saw a picture of myself standing in the aforementioned line. They were covering the event and took a picture of the guests in the lobby. When I saw the photo, I was sad to see myself, head down, looking at my phone. I realized I didn't speak to the people in front of me or behind me. At the time, I was disengaged and disinterested, but now as I looked at the photograph, I noticed the sweet baby in the stroller and the mom who was by herself, waiting in front of me. What is wrong with me? I thought, "Why didn't I talk to her? She may have been longing for some much needed adult conversation . . ." This photo was a sad reminder and wake up call for how disconnected I have become in my very connected world.

As I write this, I'm reminded that divine appointments happen when we least expect them, so we have to be engaged. A few years ago, Jason and I went to dinner at a steakhouse to celebrate our anniversary. We had a friendly waiter with whom we struck up a conversation. Even though it was a busy night, he was more than happy to talk with us. He mentioned that he was waiting tables, but it was temporary; this wasn't what he wanted to do forever. When he found out that Jason was a prior Marine, he really opened up.

"For my whole life, my dream was to be in the Marine Corps," he said. "As soon as I graduated from high school, I enlisted and went to boot camp. Everyone was miserable, but I wasn't. I didn't mind boot camp because my dream of being a Marine was becoming a reality . . . and I almost was . . ." his voice trailed off.

"What happened?" Jason asked.

"I had a small seizure the day before I was to graduate. I'd only had one epileptic incident when I was little, and it never happened again, so I didn't put that information on my medical questionnaire when I enlisted. Needless to say, my dream turned into a nightmare when instead of receiving the honor of becoming a Marine, I was sent home for fraudulent enlistment."

Our hearts broke for our waiter, who still showed the pain of this experience in his eyes. He went on to say how things seemed to go from bad to worse once he returned home, and he didn't have much hope in the future. Jason was able to speak to him about a previous experience he had in the Marine Corps and how his worst day turned out to be a blessing in disguise. He explained: "I used to consider myself a fighter pilot who just happened to be Christian, but after being involved in an accident in the Harrier, and being grounded from flying until the investigation was over, I realized an important truth—I am a Christian who just happens to be a fighter pilot. Flying jets is something that I do, but it does not define who I am."

The waiter was listening intently, but we knew he had to check on his other tables, so Jason gave him his business card and told him he was welcome to call him anytime.

Two weeks later Jason got a call: "I don't know if you remember me or not, but I was your waiter at the Keg steakhouse. I just wanted you to know that when I went home that evening, I told my wife about our conversation, and I said we should go to church the next morning. We did. During the service the pastor was speaking in military terms, and everything he was saying felt like he was talking to me personally. I wanted you to know that I prayed to receive Jesus during that service—and it feels like a weight has been lifted from me. I am no longer carrying my burdens."

Isn't God amazing! He knew our waiter was hurting, so he put someone he would listen to in his section as He orchestrated this divine appointment. But what if we were messing with our phones—disinterested and disengaged? I believe God would have found someone else to talk to him, but we would have missed out on the blessing of being part of a miracle.

I wonder how many miracles I have missed out on because I wasn't paying attention or would rather talk to someone via Facebook then with someone face to face. Oh the irony of social media! Maybe it should be called anti-social media. I can't tell you how many times I've had to tell my daughters to put their phones down and talk to the people who they are actually with. My request is usually met with resistance as they begrudgingly obey. I recently read an article about an exasperated mom who made a basket to collect everyone's phone before they sat down to dinner. On the front of the basket it said, "Wherever you are, be all there." What good advice for all of us.

In light of this, I plan to practice the art of "being all there" and engaging with the people God puts in my path. Jason says when I am messing with my phone, I have low SA (situational awareness). Not only am I being anti-social, but when I am in a public place, having low SA is dangerous as well. This requires a great amount of effort and intentionality to change.

My prayer for everyone reading this is that they would have high SA—both situational and spiritual awareness. Stay engaged, interested, and observant as you wait expectantly for divine appointments. Let's turn the tide and be purposeful to stay truly connected in our connected world.

Wherever you are, be all there.

"...but sanctify Christ as Lord in your hearts, always being ready to make a defense to everyone who asks you to give an account for the hope that is in you, yet with gentleness and reverence." (1 Peter 3:15)

Pause and Reflect

- Put your phone down and ask God to open your eyes to the miracles and wonder all around you. Ask Him to help you to be fully present and engaged. Pray to have high S.A.!

Chapter 27

A High Calling

What's your calling? It might be using your God-given gifts to serve others in one way or another, or it may be to participate in building a business, missions, or teaching kids. Whatever it is, stop to think about it.

Raising kids has been great training for the races I've participated in because before my girls were old enough to drive, it seemed as if I were always racing them somewhere. From sporting events to school, I was always on the run.

On one particular morning when my oldest daughter, Marissa, was about twelve years old, I dropped her off at her middle school. She hurriedly jumped out of the car so she could get to class on time. As I started to pull away, I realized I didn't pray for her or kiss her or anything before she got out of the car because we were running late. So in order to make up for my less than stellar parenting, I rolled the window down and, like a Chevy Chase movie, I yelled, "Marissa! Remember, what is impossible with man, is possible with God! Luke 18:27."

She cringed as she rushed into the building, pretending that she didn't know me. I momentarily forgot that she was going through the embarrassed of her parents phase, and my screaming scripture out the window probably didn't help out my cause.

As I drove home, I started feeling guilty for not honoring God's word the way I should. What kind of message was I sending by yelling a Bible verse out of my car window almost as an afterthought? I was worried that all I accomplished was embarrassing both Marissa and Jesus!

Parenting isn't for the faint of heart, I thought, as I pulled into my driveway. I could only pray that God would honor my effort and give me another chance to improve. At the end of the day, I went to pick Marissa up from school and wondered what she was going to say. As she got into the front seat of the car, I noticed she was holding a wooden whale figure in her hand.

"Mom, guess what? I made this whale in my wood shop class all by myself!" she said excitedly.

"That's great," I responded not understanding the high level of her enthusiasm.

"You don't understand," she went on to say, "I was terrified of the band saw tool I needed to use. I thought if I tried, I would cut my fingers off or something. Mom, I was going to quit and just get an F, but then I remembered what you yelled at me this morning, 'What is impossible with man, is possible with God,' so I prayed and asked God to help me do the impossible—and He did! Look at my whale!"

Her excitement became mine as I thanked God for being so awesome. He knew my intentions were good, and He honored my efforts. I love that He uses imperfect people to accomplish His perfect will. That day, I realized the power of His word. It is powerful and sharp, and will not return void, but will accomplish the purpose for which He sends it—even when it's screamed by a frazzled mom out of the window of a car!

Like I said earlier, parenting isn't for the faint of heart. God entrusts us with the great privilege of raising children, but along with that comes a huge responsibility. We sometimes worry that we are going to mess up and fail at the most important job in the world.

When Marissa was born and I was getting ready to leave the hospital with her, I remember thinking, "Are they just going to let me take her home? I don't even know what I am doing!" But they trusted that I would figure it out. In the same way, God trusts parents enough to let us have the honor of leading and guiding the children He has loaned us. We aren't adequate in ourselves for this privilege but He is.

Knowing this, we can rest as we look to the best Father in the world to help us out—He can turn our imperfect yet good intentions into a beautiful high calling!

"For the word of God is alive and active. Sharper than any double-edged sword, it penetrates even to dividing soul and spirit, joints and marrow; it judges the thoughts and attitudes of the heart." (Hebrews 4:12)

". . . My word that goes out from my mouth: It will not return to me empty, but will accomplish what I desire and achieve the purpose for which I sent it." (Isaiah 55:11)

Pause and Reflect

- Whatever your calling is in this season of life, do it to the best of your ability. Teach your children scripture, understanding that God's word never returns void but will accomplish its purpose.

Chapter 28

Arrows

One of the best pieces of parenting advice I've received happened on an airplane fifteen years ago. I was in the not-so-coveted middle seat, with strangers on both sides of me. The man to the right of me started making small talk about the flight, where he was headed and why. I asked him what he did for a living, and he replied, "I'm a child psychologist."

"Oh good!" I exclaimed, "because I have a question for you!" I can't remember what my parenting question was, but I do remember his response.

"Well, before I try and answer your question, let me start by asking you a question first. Are you trying to raise a child, or are you trying to raise an adult?"

Without thinking, I responded with, "I'm raising a child."

He went on to say, "Then carry on, continue doing what you're doing, and you will be successful in raising a child. However, your job as a parent is to raise a well-functioning adult who, if you do your job correctly, will be a contributing member of society who doesn't need you in order to survive." He went on to say that many well-meaning parents do everything for their kids and in effect stunt their growth and delay the maturing process. In their attempts to help, they do the opposite and enable their children to become needy and dependent.

That five-minute conversation changed the course of how I had been parenting, and I'm so glad I didn't miss it. I say that because since the advent of iPods and smartphones, I wonder if that exchange would have taken place today in our tuned-out society. I'm just as guilty as the next person, so I wonder how many life-changing conversations I've missed—but I digress.

After that day, I purposed in my heart to not raise grown-up children, so I took that man's words seriously. Now, I don't think I'll get this parenting thing down perfectly on this side of eternity, but with three daughters with five and six years between each, my husband and I have been able to see (by trial and error) what has and hasn't worked for us over the years. Below is a list of what we allowed and what we didn't.

Allowed

Allow them to do things for themselves. Allow them the pride they feel when they do those things by themselves. Allow them to fail. Allow them to experience consequences while they are young and the stakes aren't as high. Allow them to make mistakes. Allow them grace. Allow them to try again. Allow them to be responsible. Allow them to take responsibility for their actions. Allow them to try new things. Allow them to struggle because they are getting stronger and growing in the process. Allow them to get frustrated but not give up. Allow them to problem solve.

Allow them to give back to society by taking them on mission trips, church-led activities, or by volunteering at nonprofit organizations. Allow them the joy that comes from serving and giving to others. Allow them to want something. Allow them to plan, dream, and strategize on how they are going to get it. Allow them the thrill of finally getting the thing they were allowed to want for. Allow them to ask questions. Allow them to be curious and full of wonder. Allow them to have their own dreams. Allow them to be kids, while at the same time guiding them toward adulthood.

Not Allowed

Don't allow them to be lazy. Don't allow them to make excuses—if you do, that is the only thing they will ever be good at. Don't allow them to blame others. Don't allow them to be disrespectful. Don't allow them to have an entitlement mentality. Don't allow them to make their own rules because that's not how life works. Don't allow them to talk back—if they don't respect you, they won't respect anyone in authority. Don't allow them to be late without a good reason—it teaches them that their time is more valuable than others. Don't allow them to roll their eyes at you; it shows contempt.

Don't allow them to be selfish. Don't allow them to usurp your role as a parent; you're not equals at this time in their life. Don't allow them to go to bed without kissing them and telling them how much you love them. Don't allow them to learn about God on their own, but rather teach them scripture, take them to church, talk to them about the Bible, and tell them your story. Don't allow the few precious moments you have with them as children to be wasted by chasing things that won't matter for eternity. Don't allow the world to parent your children by giving them unrestricted access to it. Don't allow them to talk badly about themselves or others. Don't allow a day to go by where you don't hug and love the children God has entrusted to your care.

This requires a great amount of intentionality, but it's worth it. It's easy to allow them to do things if we are good parents and truly love our kids selflessly, but it's hard to be intentional about discipline and boundaries. For other parents, the discipline is easy, but the inspiration isn't. What are your core family values? Can your children answer that question? If they can't, it's time to sit down with them and think about it and make a list.

Being a parent is an amazing privilege—and with that privilege comes an amazing responsibility. We wonder if we are adequate for such things, and we're not. Fortunately, we have a perfect Father who is. His mercies are new every morning and His grace is sufficient.

He allows us to make mistakes, He allows us to try again, He allows us to ask questions, and He allows us the joy of being a parent. He allows us to struggle so that we may experience His power. He allows us to have a free will. He allows those, who have put their faith in Christ, to be called children of God. He won't allow us to disrespect His commandments or laws that protect us (the law of gravity is very unforgiving). He won't allow us to usurp His authority—we are not His equal. He won't allow a day to go by where He isn't concerned and engaged in every detail of our life. He won't allow His children to ever escape His notice, and He won't allow us to be tempted beyond what we can handle but will provide the strength to do the right thing. He is a forgiving God, but He won't allow us to be exempt from the consequences of our choices. He won't allow us to walk alone.

He understands how hard and how rewarding being a parent is. The Bible says, "Like arrows in the hand of a warrior, so are the children of one's youth" (Psalm 127:4). Being a warrior isn't easy or for the faint of heart, so we must look to our Heavenly Father for guidance and strength. How we train up our children is critical because we are sending them into a future entrusted to their care. What an amazing privilege. What an amazing responsibility.

"Train up a child in the way he should go, even when he is old he will not depart from it." (Proverbs 22:6)

"Like arrows in the hand of a warrior, so are the children of one's youth." (Psalm 127:4)

Pause and Reflect

- Are you trying to raise a child or an adult? In what areas are you doing too much for your kids?
- What are your core family values?

Chapter 29

To Do or Not to Do?

Have you noticed that we have more time-saving devices than any other generation yet never seem to have any extra time? We are more frazzled, hectic, and overwhelmed than ever before and wonder if there is a solution to the madness.

Years ago when I was freelancing out of my house, I was frantically going through my desk drawers, trying to find a notebook that had important contact info I needed to complete a graphic design job that was due to the printer that day. I was frantic because, once again, I overextended myself and took on a task that I should have turned down.

As I was going through my papers, I came across a to-do list that my then eight-year-old daughter Savanna had written. I sat down and read it, blown away by the wisdom displayed. I remember thinking, wow, if I would take the time to plan out my day like this, I wouldn't be half as stressed as I was, and life would be so much easier.

Below are the tasks on Savanna's list:

- Read—0
- Draw, color—5
- Art—10
- Look for money—29
- Sleep—2
- Make up dance—0
- Eat—15

- Watch TV—4
- Jump—4
- Math—0
- Play with Skyler—0
- Bathroom—3
- Play on computer—0
- Think—0

After studying her to-do list, I decided to break it down and try to practice the same principles.

Allocate Time

The first thing I noticed about Savanna's list is that she put time limits next to each task. I'm still not sure if I understand her system (was it seconds, minutes, hours? Did her numbers reflect how much time she allocated or the time she actually spent on each task?) Regardless of this, I love the discipline of allocating time limits for our activities. This is so important because it keeps us from procrastinating or getting sidetracked. Have you ever noticed how much more is accomplished on days that are full, as opposed to when we have a lot of time on our hands? We find the time when we have to get things done. We only have so many hours in our day, so time limits are necessary. Remember, lost time is never found again, so we should use it wisely.

On that same note, if we have goals included on our lists, then a date should be set on when we plan to accomplish them. Goals are merely dreams if we don't do this. Dreams are easy and can go on forever, but our goals should be action-oriented with a specific time frame. Of course, the dates can change if they have to, but at least have a general timeline.

Prioritize and Minimize

I was impressed with how Savanna prioritized what she wanted to do. Usually the first thing we write on our lists is the most important. It would make life easier if we would prioritize what really needs to be done in the order of importance. I love how all the tasks on her list were attainable. I've found frustration reigns when I overload my to-do list. Instead of feeling a sense of accomplishment at the end of the day, I feel defeated and focus on what I wasn't able to complete. I've since learned to not put it on the list if it is not important or it can wait.

I found that I need to be intentional about creating "margin" space in my life. Consider the words on this page. If the letters covered the whole page, extending to the edges with no white space, it would stress your eyes out! The same is true when we pack our schedules so full that we don't have time to do things like, I don't know, think or relax or something else that we really want to do. Stress is then inevitable. Stress kills, and it needs to be taken seriously. Remember, you don't have to attend every event you are invited to; it is okay to say no.

Emotional, Physical, Intellectual, Occupational, Spiritual, and Social Tasks

My eight-year-old had it figured out—in fact, her list looked a lot like the *Six Dimensional Wellness model* used in many colleges. She covered all aspects of life into her list: emotional, physical, intellectual, occupational, social, and spiritual.

Emotional Tasks

Think—I love this. How many of us sit down and take time to just think (Pay no attention that she allocated a 0 next to this one). In this busy world of noise and activity, it would serve our souls well to just be still. Be forewarned that this is not an easy task. In our overstimulated, noisy, nonstop world, the art of being quiet is not comfortable. Putting our phones down, turning off the radio, TV, and so on and doing nothing but think is a dying practice that we should fight to reclaim. God tells us that we should be still and know that He is God (Psalm 46:10). If God says it, it must be important!

Social Tasks

Play with Skyler—I loved that Savanna realized it was important to make time for relationships and play with her little sister. Even though our family and friends are important to us, it is easy to overlook them because we know they love us unconditionally. Something that has helped me in this area is a quote I read a few years back that reminds us to "Live your life, focusing on those who will cry the hardest at your funeral."

Occupational Tasks

Look for money—Since Savanna was only eight, I guess she considered looking for money as her job description! She also realized her job was going to take up most of her day, so she put the highest number next to this one. She was correct because work does consume the majority of our time. Since this is the case, we should always try and do our very best at our jobs. The Bible reminds us to work as if working for the Lord and not for man (Colossians 3:23). This is important because how we spend our moments is how we spend our lives.

Intellectual Tasks

Draw, color, art, and math—Exercising our brains is as important as exercising our bodies. When kids are little, they choose to do these things because it is fun, not realizing it is also a healthy thing to do. We should be intentional and set time aside every day to learn something new, be creative, journal, or even color or draw.

Never, never, never stop learning!

Physical Tasks

Jump—Just jump. I smile every time I read this on Savanna's list. It was so important to her that it got a 4 next to it. We should have the same thing on our list, but if jumping isn't your thing, you can fill in the blank: go to the gym, go for a run, take a walk, go swimming, and so forth. Physical exercise helps keep us healthy, makes us feel better about ourselves, provides a natural high (I call endorphins God's natural painkiller), and helps us to sleep better at night. Don't overlook exercise when your list is full; it is as important as everything else if not more. Stay active and like a kid, consider it fun, not something that you dread.

Make up a dance—if any of the above exercise suggestions sound horrible, then make up a dance.

Spiritual Tasks

Read—Savanna realized the importance of reading but didn't seem to get around to it on this particular day! For me, I put read in the spiritual category because as a Christian, I start each day by reading the Bible. In a world that has gone crazy, it is my lifeline. I am reminded, even before my day starts, that God is in control in a world that seems out of control, and nothing takes Him by surprise. The news scares us with war, disease, economic collapse, and so on, but I don't have to be consumed by fear because I choose to have faith consume that space. Starting each day with God's word is something I look forward to every morning. It is a *get to* on my to-do list.

What's on yours?

I hope my daughter's list helps you the way it has helped me over the years. Companies that are successful usually have a mission statement. They know what they want to accomplish, how they are going to accomplish it, and when they plan on accomplishing it. For us to be successful in life, we each need to manage our choices and set clear goals for what we want. As quoted by Michael Altshuler, "The bad news is that time flies. The good news is you're the pilot." Make your list well!

"Therefore be careful how you walk, not as unwise men but as wise, making the most of your time, because the days are evil. So then do not be foolish, but understand what the will of the Lord is." (Ephesians 5:15–17)

Pause and Reflect

- Dreams are easy and can go on forever, but our goals should be action-oriented with a specific time frame. Put a date on your calendar on when you want to accomplish your goal. Celebrate when you do!

Chapter 30

Don't Be a Flipper

No matter who we are in life, it's important to take a stand for what you believe in and stand firmly rooted. Do the right thing, the right way, and everything will work out. Do the right thing the right way even if it costs you something or is painful. We don't compromise because the road is challenging. Whether we like it or not, as Christians, we represent Jesus. This can be hard when we are having a bad day and wish that we could go incognito for a while.

I signed up for the Houston Marathon six months in advance, not anticipating getting sick a week prior to the event. I had come down with a chest cold that was relentless and persistent—good qualities for a marathon runner but not a cold! I figured I would just show up at the expo where you pick up your race packet, and have them switch my full marathon bib for the half marathon one. My friend Toni was with me, and after our Boston Marathon experience, she said she was not going to leave my side and would change her bib as well. When we tried to switch from the full marathon to the half marathon, the volunteer at the expo told us we couldn't do that since we waited until the last minute. She went on to say that nothing was stopping us from only running the half; we would just have to do it with the bibs that were already assigned to us.

On race morning, I woke up coughing, and I just didn't feel good. I comforted myself by remembering that I was only going to run half of the 26.2 mile run. Toni and I put on our matching

Team 4:13 shirts we purchased for this race and made our way to the starting line. I knew it was going to be a long day when only ten minutes into the run, Toni got ahead of me. She thought I would stay right behind her, but that wasn't happening. She looked back and saw that I wasn't with her so she ran back to me.

"What are you doing?" She asked.

I laughed, "This is it—this is as fast as my legs have agreed to run."

It felt like I was stuck in second gear! Toni, on the other hand, felt great but true to her word, she stayed with me.

Normally, when we are running marathons, we are so focused on running for time that we miss out on everything around us but not on this day. Since we weren't pushing ourselves, we were able to enjoy the race, high-five the kids and spectators along the course, and even stop at a prayer tent that was set up for anyone who needed some divine assistance. Since I was feeling bad, I gladly stopped and ask them to pray for me. I needed all the help I could get! As we ran together, spectators noticed our shirts and encouraged us by shouting affirmations like "Good job! Go Team 4:13!" and "Yay, Team 4:13! Way to go!"

I loved their words, and I felt extreme gratitude that I was able to appreciate it. I usually try and run as fast I can. I'm competitive, and this is what you train for, so why waste it? I love to push myself to reach my goals. But on this day, everything was uncommon. Normally when I raced, I was so focused on speed that I missed out on everything around me except for the ground right under my feet.

In Houston, although I loved being able to take it all in and slow down a bit, I was still not feeling well and was looking forward to being done. I knew I only had to endure it for a little while longer, then I would be able to start running back to the finish line. About nine miles into the run, we got to a sign on the course that told half marathon runners to turn left and full marathon runners go straight. "Thank you, Lord," I said as we approached the sign. That was when I heard another person scream,

"Go Team 4:13! You can do it!"

I immediately stopped running because I felt like I was going to get sick. The back of our shirts said, Team 4:13 with the verse from

Philippians, "I can do all things through Christ who strengthens me" in big, bold letters underneath it.

"Toni, Oh no! We can't quit; we can't turn left," I cried.

"What are you talking about? We agreed to just do the half," she asked with a "you've got to be kidding me" look on her face.

"I know I said that, but we have full marathon bibs with shirts that say that we can do all things through Christ who strengthens us. If we turn left and run with the half marathon group, everyone is going to notice. Ugh. . . . We didn't think this through this morning."

I knew the right thing to do was finish the full marathon since I chose to represent Jesus the moment I put that shirt on, but since nothing within me wanted to run one step further—let alone seventeen more miles, I panicked.

"Do you have coin? I desperately asked Toni.

"No, why?"

"Well, choosing lots is in the Bible isn't it? I mean it's biblical, right? Maybe God doesn't want me to run any further in my sickened state, so if I flip a coin and it lands on heads, that means He wants me to run; if it lands on tails, He doesn't." Okay, okay, before you laugh here or think I'm totally crazy, I know you've done something just as crazy in your own life. Humans will go to great lengths to avoid making a decision that's difficult. Running the whole marathon would be difficult. It wasn't my finest Christian moment since I already knew that the right thing to do would be just to suck it up, work hard, stay committed, and finish the race, but I was looking for any excuse not to. Since neither one of us had a coin, I decided the next best thing would be a gel pack (nutrition you consume during the race).

"If it lands on the ingredients side, that means we run the half marathon. If it lands on the front side, we run the full," I said as I threw the gel packet into the air.

It landed face up.

"Two out of three," we cried in unison.

Again, it landed face up.

Looking back now, I can't imagine what the spectators were thinking as they watched us freaking out, throwing gel packets in the air over and over again. The whole thing went on for about three minutes until we realized we were going to complete another marathon that day. It was a defining moment.

As we began to run straight and follow the rest of the full marathon group, I realized what a good friend Toni was to me. She wanted to turn left as much as I did but had promised to stay by my side. Blessing always follows obedience, and we both found the strength to endure. The seventeen miles we still had to run weren't easy, but it wasn't as terrible as we thought it would be. In fact, Toni was feeling so good that she would run ahead of me then turn around to come back and get me. I told her she should get an ultra-marathon medal since she was running a lot further than 26.2 miles!

Along the way, we saw a friend who was hurting, and we were able to walk with her for a little bit and encourage her along the way. We were also able to happily acknowledge the spectators that continued to yell, "Go Team 4:13" with sincere smiles on our faces. Joy also follows obedience.

When we got to the finish line, we looked at our time and realized we ran it in four hours and sixteen minutes. Ironically, if I had not stopped to flip gel packs for three minutes, our time would have been 4:13! We were both happy that we made the decision to run the full marathon, and to this day, it is one of our favorite marathon memories. But it got even better when a fellow runner approached us and said, "I just wanted to thank you girls. I was running near you at mile 24."

"For what?" we responded.

"Well, I have been struggling with my walk with the Lord for a while. I read the back of your shirts. Then I saw how your friend would always come back for you. She never let you out of her sight." For some reason, I needed to see this."

What beautiful confirmation for completing the full run—we really were representing Jesus, even though we didn't know it at the time. I'm glad God impressed it on his heart to tell us this. It was a kiss from God for sure! In our life walk, we don't always see the complete picture, but it's nice when God reveals glimpses that give us affirmation. Press on, warrior, press on. Seeing the fruit of obedience always gives me confidence to persevere.

God didn't stop at one kiss; we looked ahead of us and saw a friend who had just completed his very first marathon. He was standing by himself in an area where only participants could be. We had the privilege of making a big deal about his accomplishment. We took his picture, tagged him on Facebook, and bragged about what a great job he did for all his friends and family to see. A joy shared is twice as great!

Whenever I remember this story, I am reminded that a shirt shouldn't be what motivates me to represent Jesus well. I want my life to reflect His character at all times. Unfortunately, I've proven time and time again that I am not always perfect in this area. As you've read in this story, one minute I trust His will for me completely, the next I'm flipping gel packets to get my way. The good news is He knows my heart and that I'm trying my best. I have great assurance in knowing that perfect people don't get into heaven—forgiven people do.

"For we are his workmanship, created in Christ Jesus for good works, which God prepared beforehand, that we should walk in them." (Ephesians 2:10)

Pause and Reflect

- As Christians, we represent Jesus to a world that is watching everything we say and do. Pray that God will strengthen you to be a good reflection of Him.

Chapter 31

Gifts

I talk a lot in this book about trust and faith because they are the ingredients that create the abundant life God intends for us to have. Jesus says He comes to give us life and life to the full (John 10:10). I'm a visual learner, so when I think about this verse, I envision gifts under a Christmas tree. The big box is the gift of salvation we receive when we put our trust in Christ—the gift of eternal life. God's word tells us in Ephesians 2:8 that "it is by grace you have been saved through faith; and that not of yourselves, it is the gift of God." This gift can't be earned or bought. It costs us nothing, but it cost Jesus everything. Our part is simply to receive this priceless gift.

After that gift has been opened, there are hundreds of other presents that contain blessings Jesus purchased for us. Unfortunately, many Christians don't open these gifts because there are certain requirements that must be met. For example, one of the boxes contains an extra measure of faith. The only problem is that it takes faith to open the box! So how does anyone open it? You use the measure of faith you currently have, no matter how small, and in return you are rewarded with a bigger, bolder, better faith. This process will continue as we keep opening the faith packages. We are taken from faith to faith, but we must start the process by opening that first gift of faith.

Another gift God can't wait for us to open contains wisdom. The instructions on how to open this package are located in the Bible. As you read, memorize, and apply scripture, the gift of wisdom is given to you.

Do you want to open the gift that contains trust? Then you must be willing to cling to God at all times and not curse. To cling or curse is a choice we each have to make. The ones who cling, no matter what, find their trust in God increases. They have empirical data that He is trustworthy.

A beautiful package with a tag that says Peace is opened when our minds are fixed on Jesus and not our problems. When we put our trust in Him and thank Him for everything He has already provided, peace is the gift we receive that no amount of money can purchase. God's promise in Isaiah 26:3 belongs to all who will open this gift: "The steadfast of mind You will keep in perfect peace because he trusts in You."

Do you want God to make you stronger? This gift is yours for the taking, but you must do hard things in order to open it. You must be willing to go outside your comfort zone, be steadfast, and endure as a good soldier of Christ. Be obedient in pursuing this gift, and you will go from strength to strength.

Do you want to open the gift of abundance? It's yours the moment you are faithful and give. God even challenges us to test Him in this area: "'Bring the whole tithe into the storehouse, so that there may be food in my house, and test me now in this,' says the LORD of hosts, 'if I will not open the windows of heaven for you and pour down for you a blessing until it overflows'" (Malachi 3:10). You will find, like I have, that it is impossible to outgive God. I love His economy!

I could go on and on, but I think the point has been made. I encourage you not to let the enemy of your soul keep you from receiving what belongs to you. I pray you have the faith to open each and every gift that God has for you. Don't let the enemy keep you from what is yours. His *raison d'être* is to steal, kill, and destroy—don't let him! Remember that the only power he has over you is the power you give him. Jesus came to give us life and life to the full. We honor His sacrifice by taking the time needed to open every present He purchased on our behalf.

I want to be like kids on Christmas morning, who joyfully race to each present that has their name on it. The thought of not opening every single one would be insane. Let's take their lead and tear into every gift that is waiting for us so we can live life to the full!

"...I have come that they may have life, and have it to the full."
(John 10:10)

Pause and Reflect

- What gift do you need to open so that you may live the abundant life Jesus promises?

Chapter 32

Press On

How many times in your life have you felt like you couldn't take one step further, the road was too long, the hills were too steep, and the challenge too great? When we find ourselves defeated and distraught, relying on others is crucial. We need each other in this world, and we should never try to tough it out alone. Depending on others doesn't make us weak because together, we are strong. I saw a beautiful visual of this at a run I participated in recently.

I was six miles into a 20k trail run in Palo Duro. Known as the Grand Canyon of Texas, the Palo Duro Canyon is located near Amarillo and is the second largest canyon in the country. As I was running, I was thinking about what a beautiful, unexpected, natural wonder this place was and was so happy that I was able to experience it. Because the trails are very narrow and steep in some places, we would have the occasional "traffic jam" and have to slow down for those ahead of us. As my friend, Donna, and I were climbing one of these short but steep hills, an elderly man in front of us started to fall backwards. Fortunately, many hands caught him and pressed him forward until he made it to the top.

A kind woman stayed with him and held onto him to make sure he was okay. He didn't seem upset or embarrassed by his stumble but gratefully received help from the people surrounding him. I was thinking about how this could have been so different had no one offered a helping hand. He would have fallen backward, and since the hill was steep, it would have created a domino effect. Like Jack and Jill, we all would have tumbled down that hill. Supporting him was both considerate and smart!

I would like to say that his stumble was an anomaly, but it wasn't. Every time he tried to ascend a hill on his own, he would wobble and appear to be falling backward. He was unsteady and disoriented, completely dependent on others to help him. Trail runners are a special group of people, and I was impressed how no one seemed to care about their race time but rather chose to take turns shuffling alongside a man who needed assistance. I overheard one girl ask him if he had been a runner his whole life, and he responded by saying, "probably!" She smiled and continued to make small talk as she pushed him up the narrow trail.

I, too, was smiling as I told my friend that this man has it figured out! With uncomplaining faith, he pressed on toward the goal of the finish line. He was undeterred and never once mentioned quitting. By unashamedly receiving help from others, he became the Palo Duro rock star, surrounded by people taking turns putting their arms around him! I think quitting never occurred to him because he was never alone.

After I finished the race, I was speaking to my friend and wondered out loud if he would be able to complete the twelve-mile run? I was worried about him because I couldn't see how it would be possible for him to finish. She told me that she saw him at around mile seven and stayed by his side for at least three miles and that he didn't seem to have any desire to quit. He was proceeding as if success were inevitable! Not long after our conversation, I looked up and saw him walk past me, a lovely girl at his side, who took him to get his finisher's hat. How awesome is that? He was aware of his weakness, so he depended on others for strength. Not only did he accomplish the impossible, but he made a lot of pretty friends along the way.

Watching him put his hat on, I was reminded of my own struggle and need during a race a few years back. I had signed up for a marathon that had horrible weather conditions. It was hot, humid, and miserable. To this day, it is one of the hardest marathons I've completed, yet it gave me one of my favorite memories. Like the elderly gentleman, I found myself not able to get up a steep incline at the end of the grueling twenty-six-mile race. Not far from the finish line, I stopped, looked at Mt. Everest (which in reality was a tiny incline, but since my strength was gone, it seemed an impossible feat). My friends, Toni and Chimene, saw that I was struggling, so Toni took my hand and pulled while Chimene put her hand on my back and pushed. If it weren't for them, I would have had to crawl up that thing! Have you been in place in life where you needed both a push and a pull? Take my advice and don't try to make it to the top of your hill alone, whatever that hill may be. The reason this is one of my favorite memories is because it showed the power of unity and how the impossible became possible when I received help from others. We deny others a blessing when we stubbornly refuse help because, like I've said before, a burden shared is half as heavy and a joy shared is twice as great!

I got to see the good in humanity that day as well as during the Palo Duro Trail Run as I watched how community should be. During the trail run, one person couldn't do it alone, so everyone took turns and participated in serving and helping a fellow brother in need. His victory became all of our victories as we celebrated after seeing him cross the beautiful finish line.

We, too, have an eternal finish line we will cross someday. In the meantime, we can rest in the knowledge that we have a strong Savior who will never leave our side. We can keep going because we are never alone. We can proceed as if success were inevitable because it is. His hand is on our back, pushing us when we need it, and when it gets too tough, He promises to carry us. By depending on the strength of Jesus and not our own, victory is secured.

What struggle or hill are you climbing right now? The best way to overcome it is to encourage and help someone else. Your positive words and actions increase another person's faith and at the same time takes your mind off your own pain. When we choose to participate and be the hands and feet of Jesus by supporting others, and when needed, allowing others to support us, we can confidently enjoy the journey as we push and pull each other to a beautiful destination that will be well worth the pain in getting there!

"I press on toward the goal for the prize of the upward call of God in Christ Jesus." (Philippians 3:14)

"Like an eagle that stirs up its nest, that hovers over its young, He spread His wings and caught them, He carried them on His pinions." (Deuteronomy 32:11)

"For momentary, light affliction is producing for us an eternal weight of glory far beyond all comparison." (2 Corinthians 4:17)

Pause and Reflect

- Don't deny someone of a blessing by doing everything on your own. In what areas do you need help? God created us to need each other, so don't be afraid to both ask and receive help from others.
- Do you have uncomplaining faith? If not, remember that what we complain about tends to get worse, and what we appreciate tends to get better.

Chapter 33

A Better Plan

Most people reading this book will feel that Boston was the biggest tragedy, trial, or learning experience that happened in my life, but it's my belief that life is a series of victories and challenges, and you can learn from them all. This book isn't just about Boston but about all of the other ways we can learn and grow and learn to let go. If I had to sum it up in one word, it would be *trust*.

I've spoken a lot about endurance events in this book because I feel like they represent life in so many ways. I've been trained to trust God through all of these endeavors, but the greatest training I've ever received started when I was a teenager. As I sat alone in the doctor's office, I nervously waited for my name to be called. I wasn't there for typical teenage reasons; I wasn't getting my braces tightened or getting up to date on immunization shots. I was at an OB/GYN appointment, sitting among happy, married couples. I felt out of place, out of my comfort zone, and close to being out of my mind, wondering how any good could come from the situation I had gotten myself into.

It didn't help matters when a very distraught woman emerged from the doctor's office and into the waiting room where I was sitting. As she started to pass me, I noticed she was crying. Before she left, she stopped, turned around, looked at me, and her eyes narrowed.

She hissed, "Why? Why would God choose to give someone like you a baby and not me?" With that she slammed out of the now-silent waiting room, leaving all eyes on me.

I was embarrassed by the confrontation, but I have to confess, I was asking God the same question. Why would He choose me over someone who was ready, someone who was much more capable and qualified to be a parent? My heart began to race again as I wondered how I was going to do this.

A few months prior to this, I felt this same shame and embarrassment as I anguished over telling my family that I was pregnant. I was almost four months along, and I still could not muster the courage. Keeping this secret to myself was making me physically sick and in a constant state of anxiety, but I just couldn't bear the thought of letting everyone down. So I kept it to myself. I was scared of being an embarrassment, I was scared of the future, and I was ashamed that I had thought I was invincible. This type of thing happened to bad girls, not me. Looking back now, I see that God in His mercy had to intervene and help me peel the bandage off and share my secret.

It was on Thanksgiving Day, and the whole family was gathered around the table when I began to feel nauseous. I went to my grandma's room to lie down when my mom came in.

"What's wrong with you?" she asked.

"Nothing, Mom. I just don't feel good," I replied.

"You're not pregnant, are you?"

I couldn't believe she just asked me this question and said the words that, as hard as I tried, couldn't say. Even though I was terrified of answering in the affirmative, I knew I had to, so I sheepishly responded with, "What if I was?"

She walked out of the room, and I heard her crying. Then I heard my grandma crying, followed by my uncle's yelling. I ran to my Grandma's car where I hid on the floor praying the earth would just swallow me up. Again, I wondered how any good could come from this—I felt like I was such a disappointment. Yet, in spite of all this, it was like a heavy weight had been lifted from my shoulders because, finally, they knew. Thankfully, grace and mercy were extended after the shock had worn off, and they realized what was done was done. When my daughter Marissa was born, all the sad tears that had been shed turned to happy ones. Everyone adored her and thought she was theirs! The pain of that day was overshadowed by the joy and love felt when she entered the world.

As much as I loved my daughter, it didn't take long before the reality of adult life set in. When Marissa was six months old, I was driving home with her on a dark, cold night that perfectly represented my outlook on life when I started to despair. Marissa's dad had chosen to go down a path of drinking and partying that wasn't good for me or my daughter, and I knew that if I didn't leave him, I would be the one responsible if anything happened to her. I was so insecure in myself and so afraid of being alone that in the past, I forgave him time and time again. But on this particular night, I knew that protecting her was more important than my fear of being alone, even if that meant being alone for the rest of my life. I couldn't see a light at the end of the tunnel, I didn't have a plan, and I was tired. I pulled to the side of the road, physically, mentally, and emotionally drained as I whispered a prayer. "Lord, if you love me and have a better plan for my life than the one I have created, then I give it to you because my way isn't working out very well. I'm sorry. I'm so sorry. I can't do this on my own anymore. I need you."

I needed to know God heard my prayer, I needed something to hold on to, so I asked Him for a song to come on the radio (the only Christian song I knew at the time). God didn't disappoint as He met me in my pain. I turned on the radio, scanning through the stations, when all of a sudden, I heard the most beautiful sound in the world—the song that I asked for. From the speakers of my barely functioning radio, I heard: "Here we are in Your presence, Lifting holy hands to You, Here we are praising Jesus, For the things He's brought us through..."

At that moment, I knew with everything in my heart that God had a beautiful plan for my life. But more important, I knew that I wasn't alone and never would be again. If the God of the universe took the time to meet me in my pain, if He heard my prayer from an old, beat-up Honda Prelude on the side of a dark road, then He was with me, and He was big enough to trust. I entered my car on that horrible, terrible, beautiful, wonderful evening beat-down and depressed, but I left a brand-new person with a newfound faith that no matter what life brought or what my circumstances were, God would never leave me and He had a better plan for my life. I had a confidence in the future that I never had before. Knowing that I would never be alone again, I finally had the courage to leave a bad situation and start working on the life I envisioned for my daughter and me.

Things didn't all of the sudden become easy for me; in fact, the next few years were very hard. Being a single mom, working and going to school full-time, isn't a walk in the park, but I knew I was never alone. I had to depend on God for everything, and I realize now what a blessing in disguise that was. He was training me to trust Him. I could endure and persist when I would remember His words from Jeremiah 29:11—"For I know that plans I have for you, plans for good and not for harm to give you a future and a hope."

It is important to have faith in the future if we are to have power in the present, and that is what His word and His presence did for me. Looking back on my life today, I can say that God has been more than good to me, He did have a better plan, and has blessed my life far more than I deserve, even more than I could have asked for or even imagined.

In appreciation for all that He has done for me, I wanted to give back so I began volunteering as a counselor at a pregnancy center. For the past twelve years, I have had the privilege to be a voice for the unborn, to offer hope to young girls and women who are faced with an unplanned pregnancy, to love and encourage women who have been emotionally wounded by past abortions, and most importantly, I get to share the gospel to all who are interested in knowing where my hope comes from. They listen to me because they know that I have walked in their shoes. I have genuine compassion for them because I know how they feel. It is a great day when a woman or a young girl chooses life for her unborn child and prays to receive eternal life for herself. I thank God for entrusting me to play a part in this and allowing me to work alongside of Him.

It's been many years since I sat in that doctor's office. At the time, I was in agreement with the distraught woman, who couldn't understand why God would allow someone like me to have a baby. I wish I could run into her again. I would love to sit down with her and tell her that God has a plan for her life, a plan for good and not for harm. I would beg her to not let circumstances make her bitter but that she would instead trust God so she could be better. I would tell her that God's ways are so much higher and how He sees around corners that we don't. I would tell her that He allowed me to have a baby at that particular time because He was preparing me to someday be on the front lines of a life-and-death battle for the unborn. In His goodness, He allowed me to go through trying times, so I wouldn't put faith in my own strength but rather on His. He rescued me so that I could join His team and help rescue others. He transformed my life, and because of that I am not ashamed to boldly share the gospel. I would tell her that He is good. I would tell her to trust Him.

> "For my thoughts are not your thoughts, neither are your ways my ways," declares the Lord. "As the heavens are higher than the earth, so are my ways higher than your ways and my thoughts than your thoughts." (Isaiah 55:8–9)

Pause and Reflect

- Are you allowing the circumstances of your life to make you bitter or better?
- Memorize Jeremiah 29:11 and believe God's word when He says, "For I know the plans I have for you, plans for good and not for harm, to give you a future and a hope."

A Note to the Reader

Dear Reader,

Now that you've read this book, I hope it has encouraged you to trust God in every area of your life as you press on to know Him more. Yes, He is the God of our eternity, but He is also the God of our moments, concerned with every detail. I've learned as much, if not more, on the seemingly monotonous days as I have on the big explosion days. In fact, when God answers my little prayers, in light of all that is going on in the world, it makes me realize how big He is! Zechariah 4:10 reminds us not to despise the day of small things.

When you realize the whole universe can't contain the Lord, you know that everything is small for Him, and nothing is too difficult. I pray you trust the author of your hope as He writes a beautiful story for your life and may you point others to Him as you trust Him along the way.

—*Jennifer*